BURIED TREASURE

HIDDEN WISDOM
FROM THE
HEBREW LANGUAGE

Buried Treasure

Rabbi Daniel Lapin

Multnomah® Publishers *Sisters, Oregon*

To my faithful talmid and loyal friend,
the respected scholar and great Jew, David Klinghoffer.
Thanks to you and your lovely wife, Nika, for all your help.

Contents

FOREWORD by Michael Medved 7
INTRODUCTION 11

PART ONE: RELATIONSHIPS AND MARRIAGE

1. The Window into the Soul 15
2. Love's Enduring Foundation 21
3. No Claims on Gratitude 29
4. The Skill of Knowing 35
5. Reflections on the Laughter of a Baby 43

PART TWO: FAMILY AND CHILDREN

6. Educated Hands 55
7. A Place of Grace 63
8. Parents 71
9. Twice As Many Sisters 77
10. The Lessons of Generational Continuity 83

PART THREE: COMMUNITY AND WORK

11. The Challenge of Kindness 93
12. Settling Disputes 99
13. The Faith Factor 105
14. Adding to Our Wealth 111
15. Feel the Compulsion! 117

PART FOUR: GROWTH AND SUCCESS

16. The Road to Happiness 125
17. The Dangers of the Snooze Button 131
18. The Road to Kingship 137
19. Conquer Your Fears 143

PART FIVE: IDEAS

20. Trash or Treasure? 151
21. Mr. Silverberg's Word Puzzle 157
22. Freedom and the Obligation to Serve 165

PART SIX: SPIRITUAL LIFE

23. Ascend to the Heights 175
24. The Inner Joy of Overcoming Limits 181
25. The Source of Spiritual Energy 187
26. Maintaining Our Two Lives in Health 195
27. The Currency of Gratitude 203
28. The Way to Peace and Tranquility 209

Foreword

At age twelve, as part of the preparation for my bar mitzvah, I committed myself to an eccentric, silly, and controversial plan. Despite the disapproval of my rabbi and my Hebrew school principal, I insisted on reading through the Bible on my own—all the Hebrew Scriptures—in the all-but-impenetrable King James translation.

My teachers warned me that I'd get little from it and might be distracted from the important work of memorization and rehearsal related to the upcoming ceremony, but I stubbornly slogged forward. I read big clumps of indigestible verbiage, proudly reporting on my progress and understanding almost nothing. Meanwhile, I also attended to my main responsibilities as a bar mitzvah boy—using a tape recording to master a succession of Hebrew words in their traditional cantillation so I could publicly chant my assigned portions from the book of Genesis and Isaiah 1.

The amazing thing about this experience is that no one helped me draw the obvious connection between the minimal Hebrew reading and reciting skills my teachers emphasized and the lengthy reading of biblical translation I was determined to complete. Because I never connected these two endeavors, I remained confused and befuddled in two different languages—Hebrew and English. If only I had met Rabbi Daniel Lapin twenty years before I did!

The great gift that Rabbi Lapin bestows on all his students is a vibrant, electrifying sense of the Hebrew language as a key to understanding God's blueprint for the world. Until I began studying with Daniel in 1978, I remained appallingly ignorant about the "buried treasure" contained within the ancient tongue that the Almighty chose as His vehicle for first communicating with His children. Without some sense of this deeper significance of Hebrew, the study of the language can seem deadly boring—as generations of bar mitzvah boys can attest. And without some knowledge of the linguistic clues, uniquely Hebraic and essential to a deeper understanding of the biblical text, long passages of Scripture can seem dry and confusing.

As you pick up this book and dig for buried treasure with Rabbi Lapin, you will get some taste of the excitement and insight that makes him one of the preeminent Jewish teachers of our generation. A mutual friend introduced us, believing we'd both benefit from the connection but not realizing that he was launching more than twenty years of warm friendship and close collaboration. I was a twenty-nine-year-old writer who had enjoyed my first bestseller and also a Jewish activist and seeker. The rabbi, passing through Southern California, was teaching physics part time; trying to escape the family business (his father and two brothers were all distinguished rabbis); hoping to avoid his parents' determination to see him safely married off; and thinking about taking his cherished sailboat on a round-the-world cruise. Instead, Daniel Lapin began teaching classes in living rooms in my old beachside neighborhood of Venice/Santa Monica, and within a few years he had drawn some four hundred students—with study sessions so crowded that eager applicants often had to be turned away.

These classes gave rise to Pacific Jewish Center, the congregation that Rabbi Lapin led for fifteen years. It was a unique institution with a single membership requirement more demanding than financial dues: In order to join, you had to commit yourself to a regular study program. The essence of that study never featured Hebrew as an ordinary language, with tedious emphasis on mastering vocabulary, grammar, or conversational sentences like "Do you know the way to the bus station in Tel Aviv?" Instead, Rabbi Lapin always used Hebrew as a unique, precious window into the mind of God and as a necessary pathway into the mountainous accumulation of more than 3000 years of Jewish wisdom and tradition. That tradition emphasizes the joys of family, of course, along with the importance of intellectual and spiritual fulfillment.

In his classes the rabbi acquired one particularly brilliant and challenging student from Brooklyn. Fortunately, I succeeded in persuading him to make an exception to his sensible rule that he never become socially involved with female members of the congregation. As a result of this flexibility, Susan Friedberg soon became Susan Lapin and has joined the rabbi in raising seven remarkable (and homeschooled!) children to carry on the traditions of their people and their families.

In more recent years, Rabbi Lapin has performed a priceless service in making some of this information accessible to Christians as well as Jews. I've been privileged to attend some of his wildly popular Biblical Blueprint lectures in Seattle—festive events that draw audiences representing every religious tradition, united only by their resolve to enrich their understanding by taking Hebrew Scripture and Jewish tradition seriously.

The book you will be reading reflects the same energizing approach that has changed the lives of so many of Rabbi Lapin's students over the years. Its approach is unafraid to employ some of the author's wide-ranging secular education to elucidate and illuminate Jewish tradition. Similarly, it uses timeless religious insight, passed down from father to son for one hundred generations, to measure and judge our contemporary world.

I know in the most intimate way that Rabbi Lapin can make the Hebrew language come alive in a truly life-changing manner. Some years ago, a trendy, well-established journalist was commissioned by a glossy magazine to interview the rabbi for an article titled "The Jewish Revival in California." She found herself so intrigued by his approach that she began sitting in on his classes—including one group of notoriously curmudgeonly scientists and professionals known as The Skeptics Group. The writer became so excited by the substance the rabbi offered, and particularly his revelations about Hebrew as God's language, that she renewed her own dormant Jewish heritage and became an active member of our congregation. Diane also became my wife in 1985, and in a real sense I owe my marriage and our three kids to the effectiveness of Rabbi Lapin's teaching. And yes, of course he presided at our wedding.

I had reason to celebrate nearly sixteen years ago, but now there is additional cause for rejoicing—as with his book Rabbi Daniel Lapin explores mysteries, reveals secrets, upholds timeless truths, and unearths buried treasure to a larger audience than ever before.

You are fortunate to now take part in the adventure!

MICHAEL MEDVED
SEATTLE, WASHINGTON

Introduction

Over the years thousands of people have asked me questions about God, about relationships, about sex, about money—about almost anything you can imagine. Is this because they think I am more intelligent or better educated than they are? I doubt it. I suspect they come to me for another reason altogether. They turn to me in the same way they might turn to a cardiologist for advice about heart disease, or to a financial planner when they are ready to invest. They understand that years of learning, working with, and applying information allow people to gain expertise in certain fields.

Similarly, people have come to me with their questions because they believe that I have had exposure to a valuable branch of knowledge. I am the fortunate recipient of a three-thousand-year line of oral transmission that has been passed down from generation to generation. This vast body of ancient data reached my father, and over many years he passed much of it on to me. What is this data? The best way to explain it is a general theory of the totality of all existence—a set of theorems or permanent principles that apply everywhere and in all times. The Jewish people call it the Torah. Eventually translated into many languages, the Torah, or Bible, can be studied through a competent translation, but unfortunately, in this fashion one obtains only a microscopic morsel of the available wisdom. This is because the message is bound up with the language.

It was Marshal McLuhon who made famous the phrase "The medium is the message," and movies and television have proved his phrase to be true. If I were to inform you that a truly uplifting and noble message is available in a recently released form of entertainment and I asked you to guess whether it was to be found in a book or a movie, what would you say? I think there is a pretty good chance that you would think for a moment and then say to yourself, "I don't think I have seen too many movies with uplifting and noble messages, whereas I have read books like that." You would probably guess that I was referring to a book, and you would be right. The medium is part of the message and so is the language in which it is communicated.

We tend to think of French as the language of romance, whereas Russian lends itself to brooding epics about the darker side of human nature. Hebrew, the language first spoken by Adam, and the language in which the Torah was given, is the language of ancient wisdom.

While English, like most languages, employs grammar rules that keep changing, Hebrew's rules of grammar are fixed. In English, many antiquated usages have long been abandoned while conventions that Shakespeare would never recognize are commonplace. Not so in Hebrew. The reason for this stability is that Hebrew's grammar rules are no more than an attempt to identify the patterns of structure and syntax found in the Torah. What is even more striking is that Hebrew's syntax is not arbitrary, and its word structure is not capricious. We understand and are thrilled by the logic that links the elegance of the language to the infinite wisdom of its Creator.

This book reveals some of the fundamental truths of the Torah without requiring the reader to master the Hebrew language. Like me, you may sometimes wonder whether the latest modern theories about the things that ultimately count are really reliable. Each day, experts churn out ever more radical notions about how we ought best to live our lives. Each day the media hype these notions as fail-safe guides by which to totally rearrange our priorities. Seldom does anyone mention the inconvenient fact that today's pronouncements invariably contradict yesterday's. I intend this book for readers who suspect that the more things change, the more we need to depend upon those things that never change.

Citing trends of past decades, young couples have been told that they should have no children, or at most one, and also that at least two children are needed for optimum emotional health. Day care has been invoked as the surest way to raise well-adjusted children. A little while later it is blamed for physical and psychological damage. Remaining committed to one spouse and one employer were each recommended and subsequently discouraged. Not to mention the diet fad of the month. All these contradictory pieces of advice were uttered, as if from Mount Olympus, with great solemnity and assurance. When popular trends change, as they always do, the unfortunate people that followed the experts are often left feeling that they made a horrible mistake.

The treasure buried in the Hebrew language won't explicitly tell us how many children to have or whether to seek new employment. Neither will it eliminate the challenges of being human by announcing the direction each of us should take in the countless decisions we need to make each day. However, it will expose us to the idea that there are fundamental concepts for us to employ as we make these decisions. No engineering textbook will rob a designer of his freedom to design the most beautiful bridge of which he is capable. But it will provide him with knowledge about fundamental concepts such as gravity, the tensile strength of steel, and wind force, which he will use to build a bridge both beautiful and durable. In the same way, reading this book will never deprive anyone of free choice and independence, but hopefully it will offer insights to enable the reader to make wise decisions using eternal truths.

PART ONE

RELATIONSHIPS
AND MARRIAGE

CHAPTER ONE

The Window into the Soul

PaNiM

פנים

One day, an adviser to President Abraham Lincoln brought to the White House a man whom he thought Lincoln should appoint as a cabinet secretary. The president met with the man and interviewed him. After the guest left the White House, Lincoln called his adviser into the oval office and said, "This man won't do for the job."

"Why not?" the adviser asked.

"I don't like his face."

"B-b-but—" stammered the adviser, "that's unfair! A man can't help what his face looks like."

"You're right," the president replied. "Up to age forty, he can't. After age forty, his face is him."

It's intriguing that Lincoln fastened on the age of forty, since *kabbalah,* the tradition of mysticism in Judaism, likewise identifies forty as the age before which a personality is still in formation. In other words, a person must live through four decades to reach full maturity. But more important is Lincoln's insight into an aspect of human personality that was pointed out thousands of years earlier in the grammar of the Hebrew language.

To our modern ears, to make the statement "I don't like his face" may indeed sound unfair. But the Hebrew word for face, *PaNiM,* tells us otherwise. Of course, we should endeavor to avoid judging others superficially. But when we find ourselves in a situation where we must assess someone—for instance, when we are considering a prospective spouse, employee, or employer—the Lord's language tells us it is wise to take his or her face into consideration.

PaNiM, the countenance we turn to the outside world, also means something that might reflect almost the opposite. The same Hebrew letters, *peh-nun-yud-mem,* also spell *P'NiM,* the word for "inside." If you visit the state of Israel and wander into a government office building, you will see signs for the Ministry of the Interior, called in Hebrew the *MiSRaD Ha'PaNiM,* literally the Office of the Inside. You see, though we've all heard the old saying that "the eyes are the windows of the soul," it's closer to the truth to say that the entire face is the window of the soul.

ACTIONS IMPACT APPEARANCE

I saw this concept played out in a somewhat unusual way while I was a young rabbi in training. You have probably never had the occasion to visit a slaughterhouse, but as part of my training I had to make many such inspections. I can tell you that it was among the least pleasant aspects of my preparation.

While I had to visit these abattoirs in order to learn the many and complex laws of kosher meat preparation, it was also instructive for me to look at the faces of the employees there. I observed how rabbinically trained slaughterers, called *shochtim,* slaughtered the animals. Before killing a cow or other kosher animal, the shochtim would recite a liturgy of psalms and blessings, asking God's favor and giving Him thanks.

I used to question the need for all this praying before the simple and rather upsetting act of slaughtering an animal. It was only when I studied the faces of the nonrabbinical men employed at the slaughterhouse, those who went about their business unaccompanied by worship, that I understood.

These latter individuals *looked* like they worked in an abattoir. Their faces were dark, heavy, somewhat crudely modeled. But the constantly praying shochtim had quite a different appearance. Their faces were benign, refined, and serene. Because they wrapped this brutal job in a gentle cloth of holiness and spirituality, they were protected from the coarsening effects of what they were actually doing—namely, taking life. The faces of the shochtim taught me just how powerfully our actions eventually impact our appearance.

Needless to say, positive experiences affect our PaNiM just as negative ones do. I'm reminded of the story in the book of Exodus about Moses descending from

Mount Sinai. Having just concluded a close encounter of the ultimate kind—with God himself—it is not surprising that this experience changed his face. How could it not have done so? The Bible speaks of rays of light emanating from Moses. But the truth is that since we don't know exactly what happened to Moses during his dialogue with the Lord, we can't exactly picture what effect it would have had on Moses' appearance. Whatever the case, being the "most humble of men," Moses probably could not tolerate the fact that this exalted experience could be read so easily just by looking at him. Showing this side of himself to the world must have struck him as the opposite of humility. Yet he couldn't change his face. From then on, anyone looking at him was able to tell that he had experienced something very special.

In my rabbinical work I have come to know quite a few parents of handicapped children. I am fairly certain that I could now recognize such a parent in the street. Any mother or father who has lavished selfless love and devotion upon a child over a period of years will come to possess a face that shows it.

Learn to trust your ability to read a person's face. Will you always be accurate? Of course not, but just like riding a bicycle or making an omelette, practice will make perfect. When you encounter an individual with a truly refined-looking face, enjoy the treat. You are meeting someone special.

TREASURED WRINKLES

As we get older, no matter how much we might wish we could keep looking young, the aging of the face reflects something very positive: the acquisition of wisdom. We speak about an aged face being "wizened." This literally means that its owner has *become* wise.

A biblical tradition—or *midrash*—alludes to this. Speaking symbolically, this particular midrash tells us that before the time of the biblical patriarchs, faces didn't become visibly older. People had pretty much the same face when they entered old age that they had had as children. The message is that until the beginning of the era of Abraham, Isaac, and Jacob, opportunities to acquire wisdom (i.e., wisdom about the Creator) were scarce. Human faces back then reflected this scarcity of wisdom that matures a face. Thus, we should treasure every one of our facial wrinkles as a certificate of wisdom and understanding.

A deeper reality here is that our faces reflect more than just our mood at the moment. Over the years, with a startling, even frightening permanence, they assume features in accord with our inner selves. Maybe Lincoln was right when he observed that this tends to happen by around age forty. For some it may be earlier and for others later, but eventually we all end up with the faces we deserve.

Literature and popular culture are full of stories that reflect these principles. Take Oscar Wilde's insightful novel *The Picture of Dorian Gray*. You might remember that the plot concerns a dissolute young man who wishes never to grow old, and more to the point, never to see his corrupt lifestyle reflected in the appearance of his face. Dorian makes a bargain with the devil: Rather than his face aging and changing in accord with his behavior, a portrait of Dorian, hidden in his home, will mutate over the years as his face ought to have done. Years later, as an old yet still young-looking man, he views the portrait and is horrified to find that the terms of his bargain have been kept exactly: The face in the painting has become that of an unspeakably ugly monster.

Americans, men and women alike, spend countless hours and dollars trying to make their faces conform to a cultural ideal. Makeup, skin cream, acne medication—you name it, we use it. This is going about the task backward. Superficially, it's true that emotional and behavioral factors affect appearance as much as anything else. They can change the way we look overnight. A bad night's sleep, overindulgence in food or drink, or an upsetting night the evening before can all make us wake up the next morning with a bad outbreak of acne pimples. That bottle of ointment in the medicine cabinet can only partially correct the emotional havoc making its appearance in that form.

But a more important lesson to keep in mind, one of more permanent relevance, is that if we want to look a certain way—refined, handsome, or beautiful—we stand a better chance of doing so if we begin acting that way. We have all had the experience of meeting people who carried themselves so royally that we never realized their features were uneven or their hair less than silky. Conversely, all the beauty creams in the world can't correct the damage to our appearance caused by a nasty disposition.

OUR MANY FACES

In English we naturally speak of a person having one face. In fact, the term *two-faced* is viewed as an insult. Surprisingly, however, the Hebrew language treats the face, PaNiM, as a noun that appears only in the plural form, never in the singular. This grammatical fact about the Hebrew word reveals another fundamental truth about human beings: There is no word for the singular of *face* because no person has only one face. Each of us has many, many faces. We have one for dealing with the UPS man, one for playing with our children, another for whispering sweet nothings to our spouses, and still another for dealing with subordinates at work.

Even when dealing with each of these various people, we have many faces. Ideally, we should never get truly angry with our children. However, it would be a mistake not to recognize that sometimes we need to show an angry face to them. On other occasions we need to show a face of joy—even if, for instance, we've heard our child's riddle ten times before. It is disconcerting to try to relate to someone whose facial expressions never change according to circumstance.

The only time our facial muscles stop changing and fully relax is in death, when the expression flees the face entirely. As long as we are passionately alive, our enormously complex existence and personality can only be captured by a plural, not a singular. No matter how filled with integrity we may be, nobody can describe any one of us with only a one-dimensional depiction. This is what makes cartoon caricatures so funny. They work because the cartoon artist focuses on only one facet of his subject and highlights it disproportionately. This suggests, humorously, that the grotesque exaggeration is all there is to the victim. We laugh because we recognize that no human being can be depicted by only one drawing.

Being a person of integrity is the challenge we know it to be, because it is very difficult to reconcile all the various aspects of our personalities under one unifying umbrella. The face's many moods reflect how our very essence is not singular; instead, like the word *PaNiM,* it is plural. And this is true not only over the course of an hour or a day, but also over a lifetime. It would be weird if it were otherwise. Imagine a man whose face remained, at age sixty, what it had been when he was a boy of five. Unnerving, right?

NO TRUE HEROES

The word *PaNiM* tells us something else very useful about how to go about evaluating people. I refer to the idea of the "hero." From childhood on, we've all been encouraged to seek heroes we can emulate. I remember the aftermath of Israel's 1967 war with its surrounding Arab nations. The Jewish state was led to a seemingly miraculous victory by General Moshe Dayan, whom many Jewish school children came to view as the world's greatest Jewish hero. Dayan may well have been one of the greatest military men of the century, but he was also an adulterer and possessed many other personal frailties. Not exactly an appropriate hero for a nice Jewish boy or girl.

What *is* a hero, exactly? In a simplistic world, it's a man or woman whom we can profitably imitate in every way, by copying every aspect of his or her personality. But if we learn anything from PaNiM, it is that human beings are far more complex than the idea of a hero is prepared to concede. We have too many faces—

and not all are attractive ones—ever to be a true hero.

The most famous book ever written in Hebrew, the Bible, clearly recognizes this. There are no heroes in the Bible—as indeed there is no word for *hero* in the Hebrew language. Even the Bible's noblest and most powerful characters are flawed. Consider King Saul with his terrifying temper or King David's overreaching in his relationship with Bathsheba. Even Moses was unexceptional as a husband and father; his two sons achieved no great distinction. While each of these individuals, as well as the matriarchs and patriarchs, has specific traits well worth emulating, none are perfect. Only God is perfect.

The corollary to that idea is that even those people who have a flaw that renders them worthy of our contempt will have some strengths. People are never all good or all bad. Having multiple faces, or multiple parts to our personalities, is a consequence of being human. It is also a guarantee that none of us can ever achieve perfection in every one of our many PaNiM. Rather than causing us to be depressed by the impossibility of attaining perfection, the ancient Hebrew book of wisdom called *Pirke Avot* advises that a wise person is "he who learns from every man." In other words, even the most humble among us has at least one face from which his friends and colleagues can learn something.

These are some of the reasons that I do not believe for a moment that the Internet will eliminate travel. In no way will e-mail or even video conferencing render face-to-face meetings unnecessary. See, I just used the key phrase: *face-to-face*. Whether for business purposes or for family get-togethers, we humans absolutely need and desire to see one another's faces. Deep within us is the subconscious realization that our faces really are the windows into our souls.

CHAPTER TWO

Love's Enduring Foundation

ChoVa

חבה

My husband has just told me he doesn't love me!"

I struggled to make out what my caller was saying. She was not only distraught—the emotional pain evident in her voice—but she was also gasping for breath. I pictured her and the electric breathing apparatus to which she was hooked up most of each day. Her husband, Sam, came on the line and urged me to hurry to their home.

During my short drive to their luxurious mansion in Santa Monica, I had time to reflect on their unbelievable story.

Shortly after their marriage thirty years earlier, Miriam was stricken with polio and severely restricted in her activities due to the mechanical devices she depended on to keep her breathing. Young Sam Rosen, whose management brilliance had already caused *Time* magazine to dub him a "corporate whiz kid," was urged by his family to terminate the ill-fated union. Well-intentioned friends also gently advised him to divorce Miriam and place her in a care facility that could be paid for by an annuity that Sam would fund. That way, they reasoned, he could do the decent thing for her while preventing her misfortune from wrecking two lives instead of only one.

"So why didn't you do that?" I had asked him soon after we started a Bible study together some five years ago. In a calm and logical voice, Sam had explained that he had not seen how he could possibly follow the advice of his family and friends. After all, he had married Miriam for better or for worse, in sickness and in health; it was a commitment. Surely I could see that, he said. Humbled and amazed, I assured him that I understood perfectly.

Now, as I pulled into their driveway, I wondered what had precipitated Miriam's frantic phone call. Sam greeted me at the door. "This is one of the biggest crises of our marriage," he said. "I've never seen her so upset."

I entered Miriam's room, which always looked more like a hospital trauma center than a private bedroom.

"He doesn't look after me out of love," wailed Miriam. She pointed her finger in accusation at her husband. Sam was silent. It turned out that earlier that morning she had asked Sam why he had so selflessly and devotedly lavished such care on her for so many years. He answered as directly as he knew how—that it was his obligation to do so. Upon hearing this answer, Miriam had become inconsolable and had finally called me.

"Tell me honestly, Miriam, what is your worst nightmare?" I inquired of her once she had calmed down a little.

She answered candidly. "That Sam will tire of constantly caring for me and have me placed in a hospital for the rest of my life."

I explained to her how unreliable was a benefit received when the donor was simply responding to a feeling or an emotional reason such as love.

"If the feeling of love is the only reason Sam cares for you, Miriam, then indeed you have cause to fear your worst nightmare coming true," I explained. "Perhaps one day, any day now, Sam will wake up 'out of love.' He might search his heart and find it empty of all feelings for you. It could happen."

I went on to explain that if his care was the result of his feelings, if those feelings should ever vanish, it would be fully consistent for him to stop caring for her. I explained how fortunate she really was. Sam had only been trying to tell her that he cared for her because of an obligation that could never change, instead of a fickle feeling that could fade away and condemn her to a lonely hospital bed forever. Indeed, she had nothing to worry about.

And so for thirty-five years until the day she died, Sam cared for Miriam. He built the house in which she could move everywhere by motorized wheelchair. He had a car engineered to accommodate her wheelchair and would tenderly carry her in and out of the car as he took her with him on short business and social engagements. He revealed through his actions that he knew what the foundation of love really was.

WHAT IS LOVE, ANYWAY?

What Sam understood intuitively is that love is as much a decision as it is a feeling.

The Hebrew word for "love and affection" is *ChiBa,* based on the word for "obligation," which is *ChoVa.* How does this work? To answer that, I need to explain a few concepts about the Hebrew language, so please bear with me.

First, it's important to note that in Hebrew, the consonants *B* and *V* are the same letter. They are both the letter *beth,* the second letter of the alphabet. How do you tell the difference? If beth is written with a dot inside it, it becomes a *B,* and without the dot it is read as a *V.*

Second, vowels are interchangeable—roots of words depend only on the consonants. So for our purposes, you may safely ignore the vowels.

Thus, ChiBa is identical to ChoVa—love equals obligation.

We are once again exposed to this lesson by recalling the Hebrew word for "friend"—*ChaVeR*—in which we clearly see the root word "obligation," or ChoVa. Sam lived his life with the clear understanding that his love, affection, and yes, even friendship with Miriam were rooted in a simple concept: obligation.

Many a wife has been tormented by the following remorseless logic. Having originally accepted her boyfriend's marriage proposal because he once said "I love you," she is now stuck in a marriage that is viable only as long as these feelings of love are intact. What can a wife say when her husband demands a divorce, saying, "I no longer feel in love with you"?

If, on the other hand, their marriage is established on the basis of not only love but also promise, commitment, covenant, and obligation, the difficult moments of their relationship can be more easily endured.

A wife can respond by saying, "Look, I really am sad that you no longer feel love for me; I really am. I will do whatever I can to try to restore the love you once felt for me. However, that wasn't the basis of our marriage. We undertook permanent obligations toward each other that simply were never meant to depend upon something as unpredictable as feelings. I hope you will once again come to love me as you once did, but meanwhile our mutual obligations continue unchanged...and how we act toward one another and toward our children cannot change."

In the timeless musical *Fiddler on the Roof,* Tevya the milkman asks his wife of twenty-five years, "Golda, do you love me?"

She replies by more or less asking him in return, "What's the difference?"

She points out how they have always lived together happily. They have shared the tasks of conducting their business and raising their family successfully. Her song shows that she has grasped one essential buried treasure from the Lord's language: Love is the consequence of accepting and discharging our obligations. Call me sentimental, but I always thought it would have been nice had Golda ended her song by confirming that she was still quite overwhelmed with love and passion for her milkman husband.

Human relationships must be built upon the foundation of obligation and commitment rather than feelings. It is for this reason that the Jewish marriage contract, called a *ketubah,* contains only a list of obligations that the husband henceforth undertakes toward his wife. By accepting those obligations and by living up to them, love is indeed nurtured between the young couple. I am not saying that the feeling of love isn't important and wonderful. I am emphasizing the wisdom of the Lord's language, which insists that love that flows from obligation endures. When obligation follows love, both are doomed.

In refutation of the sentimental 1970s novel *Love Story* by Eric Segal, I would consider it dreadfully dangerous advice to declare that "Love means never having to say you're sorry." Feeling that you never owe an apology means that you never feel any obligation. When a responsible person falls down on an obligation, he apologizes profusely. No relationship exempts you from having to say you're sorry. On the contrary, failing to deliver on an obligation absolutely compels you to apologize sincerely and ask forgiveness.

AN ENDURING FRIENDSHIP

Not only does love (ChiBa) best endure when constructed upon the foundation of obligation (ChoVa), but friendship (ChaVeR) does the same. In other words, acquiring a new friend places me under new obligations. Likewise, the way to most effectively make new friends is to shoulder new obligations.

It is almost as if the Lord's language is describing a mathematical equation that can be read both forward and backward. For instance, $2 + 2 = 4$. It is just as true, even if a little obvious, that $4 = 2 + 2$. If acquiring a new friend creates new obligations for me, then it is just as true that shouldering new obligations is a way to acquire new friends. This is why, when moving to a new city, many folks immediately join volunteer groups or other civic and service-minded organizations. Assuming new obligations inevitably wins us new friends. How odd! I am actually advising you to go out of your way to identify new obligations to undertake. This may seem counterintuitive since so many people we know go through life trying to evade obligations, but assuming them is a great life strategy. Obligations are good things that have the capacity to expand the envelope of your life.

AN ANCIENT CASE STUDY

In the context of a discussion of civil law, the ancient rabbis describe a hypothetical situation that gives us some excellent insight into one aspect of friendship. In this case, Tom claims that Jerry owes him a hundred dollars. Tom insists that Jerry borrowed this sum from him last year, at exactly 2:00 P.M. on the day before the Passover holiday. Jerry denies that he ever borrowed the money from Tom.

Witnesses are found to shed light on the dispute. They say that although they cannot attest to whether Jerry ever borrowed money from Tom, they do know that he did not borrow anything from anyone at 2:00 P.M. on the day before the previous Passover holiday. The reason they know this is because at that precise moment, they happened to have been watching Jerry relieving himself in a field far away from where Tom claims the transaction took place. The legal conclusion, obviously, is that Tom's claim is disallowed.

The real question, however, is this: Why would a handbook of morality, which scrupulously avoids vulgarity, unnecessarily conjure up an image of Jerry urinating in a field? After all, the example's purpose would have been just as well served had it described Jerry plowing that same field.

Many people wrongly assume the Talmud to be thousands of pages of irrelevant rabbinic musings. They dismiss these complex discussions as having roughly the same importance as how many angels can dance on the head of a pin. Nothing could be further from the truth. In those densely packed pages that have been pored over for millennia lies a treasure trove of insights into human nature and secrets of life.

In the hypothetical story about Tom and Jerry, the important data being communicated is not whether the court determines that a legal loan was made. That is quite straightforward. The really fascinating information is about the nature of human relationships and human friendship.

The Talmud divides all human relationships into two categories: those that are sexual and those that are not sexual. Clearly, sexual activity establishes a pretty profound relationship between two people. What kind of activity, asks the Talmud, creates an equally profound relationship of a nonsexual kind between two people?

The answer: creating or assuming an obligation. In other words, in our strange example of Tom and Jerry, the two opposite ends of the spectrum of nonsexual human relationships are anchored by borrowing money at one end and by going to the bathroom at the other.

What is one of the greatest acts of goodness and friendship that one person can do for another? This may surprise you, but one of the greatest acts of kindness one can do for another is to lend him money. (Needless to say, this discussion is confined to interest-free loans.) It is not a giant act of kindness to *give* someone money, for that risks robbing the recipient of his dignity and self-respect. By contrast, a loan could allow him to acquire independence by starting his own enterprise. He could repay the loan with the proceeds and stand upon his own two feet.

Some people actually like giving money away to poor people in a form of patronage. That kind of generosity is not as great an act of kindness as is helping a person toward independence.

You will agree, I am certain, that anyone benefiting from a great act of kindness automatically incurs an obligation toward his benefactor. You may have heard the aphorisms warning against borrowing money from, or lending it to, your friends. The Talmud turns that idea on its head and suggests that you ought to make friends of those to whom you lend money.

The story is told of the great Winston Churchill who was once asked for an urgent loan by an opposing member of parliament. While enjoying a collegial friendship with the great statesman, the strapped politician had been a thorn in Churchill's professional side for years. Whatever Winston proposed, this member opposed. When Churchill voted aye, this member voted nay. When Churchill offered a reason for some national policy or another, this member refuted Churchill's argument. But as soon as Winston loaned the funds to his colleague, all opposition ceased.

For the next two months not a peep of political protest was heard from Churchill's old antagonist. Finally, one day after lunch and on the way back into the House, in front of some mutual friends, Churchill confronted his old tormentor.

"Either pay me back my money by midnight tomorrow or resume arguing and fighting with me on the floor of the House," Churchill thundered at his bewildered opponent. The man's eyes filled with tears. He hugged Winston Churchill in silent gratitude and then took his seat across the aisle, immediately resuming his diatribes against the British lion.

What about the story of Jerry relieving himself in the field? Well now, try to think of some activity you could engage in that would benefit absolutely nobody except yourself. Not easy, is it? Buying yourself ice cream? Sorry. You see, you pleased the proprietor of the ice cream store. If that were not true, he would hardly have rushed forward to help you the moment he saw you enter his store. You may well enjoy eating that ice cream, but in so doing you also pleased someone else.

One activity that truly does nothing for anyone else is going to the bathroom. We often refer to it as relieving oneself. That is appropriate since you are precisely the person the activity does relieve. It relieves nobody else. Thus, because going to the bathroom does nothing for anyone else, it also sets up no obligation with respect to anyone else; therefore it does very little for human relationships.

The Talmudic story of Tom and Jerry is there to teach us that almost everything we do each day falls somewhere on that spectrum between relieving oneself and lending money. One valuable secret of life is to organize our lives so that most of our activities resemble lending money rather than relieving ourselves. Which is to say that we will get more out of life and we will win more friends if we always seek ways to benefit others (thereby creating obligations and friendships) rather than seeking ways to relieve ourselves.

METAPHOR FOR FRIENDSHIP

So we can see that it makes sense that the Hebrew word for friend—ChaVeR, should be rooted in the Hebrew word for obligation—ChoVa. But is ChaVeR the only word for friend? Considering that God's blueprint for humanity regards friendship as so important, it would be strange were His language to have only one word to describe friendship. Well, there is a second word for friend and it is *YeDiD,* which is spelled *yud, dalet, yud, dalet.* That four-letter word is actually made up of two identical two-letter words placed one after the other. *Yud, dalet* as in YaD spells the Hebrew word for hand. So two hands next to one another mean friendship? Of course they do. Just imagine what kind of simple clip-art image you might select to symbolize friendship. Wouldn't two hands clasping one another be near the top of your list?

Now you can clearly see the probable origin of the handshake. The original tongue, the Lord's language, declares that the word for friend is two hands touching one another. How better to announce friendly intentions than to try to "touch hands"? Yes, of course, I have heard the old chestnut about people shaking hands in ancient times to ensure that neither was armed or dangerous. That story just does not make much sense to me at all. People who knew Hebrew, and in those days most educated people did, shook hands with one another as if to say, "hand-to-hand." Shaking hands with someone was tantamount to sign language for "Hello, friend."

Furthermore, since the kabalistic symbolism of the hand means, "acquiring that which the world has to offer," the word for a friend, YeDiD, has an additional important meaning and lesson. Just as my hand helps me survive by moving food and drink from the table to my mouth, so the juxtaposition of two hands to mean "friend" suggests that two friends help one another to survive and prosper. They do this by each trying to move toward the other those things he thinks his friend needs or wants. In other words, each serves as an additional hand for the other. They are like two adjacent hands. What a perfect metaphor for friendship.

Having friends is a great blessing. The rabbis of old who wrote their transmissions in *Ethics of the Fathers* advise us to always be working at acquiring a new friend. Good advice it is, and not terribly difficult to do either. First, seek out obligations to undertake. Find new and unexpected ways to help other people, even if they did not ask for your help. *Especially* if they did not ask for your help!

Some might consider it manipulative to embark on a program of finding ways to do people favors knowing that this creates obligations toward you. But just imagine asking one of the recipients of your thoughtfulness how he feels. Would he rather benefit from your good turn even though he now owes you one, or proudly spurn your assistance?

The wise person humbly and gratefully accepts any extended hand. This simple idea demonstrates the other side of the coin of friendship. In addition to seeking opportunities to benefit others and thereby create obligations, one must just as graciously accept kindness from individuals and assume obligation toward those individuals seeking to become friends. In this way, the seamless web of social connectivity grows and strengthens, allowing the blessings of friendship and love to bring happiness and prosperity to all.

CHAPTER THREE

No Claims on Gratitude

KoRBaN

קרבן

W hat does the word *sacrifice* mean to you? Does it not suggest a difficult action in which you yield or surrender something of value?

I once heard a wife hurl this grenade at her husband: "Do you know how much I have sacrificed for you?" Oddly enough, it seemed to evoke in that husband more resentment than gratitude.

You have undoubtedly met the loyal employee who feels that he has sacrificed a lot for his employer. He has worked many overtime hours and often missed family events because he felt he was needed at the office. Perhaps I'm describing you. Yet now you may feel that your sacrifices are not appreciated.

After all, if you have made a sacrifice for someone, you have a claim to some gratitude, right? Well no, not exactly. According to the Lord's language, we may be misunderstanding what a sacrifice is and what we can expect its consequences to be.

The Hebrew word for sacrifice is *KoRBaN*, and it is used extensively throughout the biblical book of Leviticus in the context of the temple's sacrificial rites. The root of the word is *KRB*, meaning "close or related." For instance, the Hebrew word for a relative is *KaRoV*. (Remember that the second letter of the alphabet, the letter *beth*, is pronounced either *V* or *B* depending on whether or not the letter contains a dot.)

On the surface this seems rather simple. The act of making a sacrifice, or in the biblical context, bringing a sacrifice, certainly does produce closeness between the one offering the sacrifice and the recipient of the sacrifice. It is important to note that we are not talking about physical proximity but about a feeling, so we need to determine who feels closer to whom as a result of making or bringing a sacrifice.

Let's start by examining biblical usage. Were sacrifices brought only in order to please or placate a vengeful deity? Hardly. If that were true, after the Temple was destroyed about two thousand years ago, the Jews would have found another venue in which to bring sacrifices and keep God happy. Nobody ever brought sacrifices to make God feel closer to him. Animals were slaughtered and burned upon the altar in order to help the worshiper feel closer to God.

Was God in trouble when the Temple was destroyed? No, the Jews were. With the loss of their Temple in Jerusalem, their chief mechanism for bringing themselves closer (KaRoV) to God, namely the sacrifice, or KoRBaN, had been rendered inoperable by the Roman destruction. Clearly, *sacrifice* is the word we use to describe a profound action that makes us feel closer to the recipient and not the other way around.

(An interesting aside: It is easy to see how the word for our twelfth element, carbon, got its name. Burning organic material such as an animal in a KoRBaN produces that familiar black substance we call *carbon*. Just say the Hebrew word for sacrifice, KoRBaN—pronounced *COREbun*—and the English word for our twelfth element, carbon, once or twice, and you will sense the connection.)

Therefore, the employee who gives his company considerably more than his position establishes no claim to his employer's gratitude. His sacrifice does not make his employer feel any closer to him; instead it guarantees that he will feel closer to his employer. For this reason people who make what they intend to be a one-time sacrifice to their companies find that it is easier to do so again later. It becomes easier and easier to sacrifice for your work because each time you do so, you come to love your work just a little more.

IN GIVING, WE RECEIVE

The wife who sees herself as sacrificing herself for her husband is mistaken if she expects gratitude for her sacrifice. Sure, all wives and husbands are obliged to demonstrate constant gratitude to their spouse. However, this is not due to sacrifice, but because an essential part of marriage is to be constantly giving.

The Hebrew word for *give* is NaTaN, a palindrome. That is to say, it reads the same forward and backward. No matter from which end you view this word, the effect is identical. This indicates that in giving, we also receive. By handing you a gift, I receive as much gratification and benefit as you do by accepting it from me. However, the motivation for giving can never be to elicit gratitude or love. Giving makes the giver love the recipient more than it makes the recipient love the giver. Bringing a sacrifice to God helped to make the ancient Israelite love his God. Likewise, when a husband helps his spouse, it makes him love her more.

A clear example of this phenomenon is the relationship between parents and children. It is rare indeed for parents to cease loving their children and reject them. Sadly, it is far more common to encounter instances of children who want little or nothing to do with their parents. I recall once stunning my radio audience when I conducted a live interview with a man who had evicted his aged parents from an apartment building he owned. "They were late with their rent money," he insisted. It would be hard to imagine the reverse situation. Just think of how many families have unmarried children in their twenties and thirties still living at home. The children are trying to save money on rent, and for the most part, parents seem happy to help.

Funnily enough, many adult children spend countless therapy sessions describing to psychologists how their parents ruined their lives. I say "funnily enough" because you would think that the nation's therapists would have waiting rooms brimming with parents eager for help with their feelings of anger toward their children. After bringing children into the world, parents could no longer take vacations at will or eat out in fancy restaurants. Money spent on baby-sitting, orthodontia, athletics, and piano lessons meant fewer dollars for parents to spend on themselves. It would seem that parents have a far more legitimate complaint against children than the other way around. Yet, we find that parents love their children more unconditionally than do children their parents.

The reason for this is quite obvious. During the eighteen or so years that a child is being raised, who makes more sacrifices for whom? During those years, parents are constantly making sacrifices for their children. The result? The parents love their children more. This is the predictable effect of sacrifice.

Giving a gift to someone causes us to love that person a little more; making a sacrifice for someone causes us to love that person a whole lot more. Why does giving have this effect on us? One reason is that we all tend to like ourselves. The more we give to someone else, the more of ourselves we have invested in that person.

Another reason is that our emotions tend to fall in line with our actions. It would be nice if we could always be such rational creatures that we always acted in accordance with how we feel. Unfortunately we don't do that. We usually act the way we really want to and then we bring our feelings into line. We find it painful when our feelings are violated by our actions. For instance, most people who have just bought a new car are not comfortable examining the possibility that they overpaid or that they made a poor choice. Having taken the action of purchasing a new car, their emotions fall in line to convince them that it was a good buy. Psychologists have a name for our tendency to try to avoid the pain caused by conflicting emotions or by a conflict between action and feeling. They call it *cognitive dissonance*.

Another example of this human tendency can be seen among ex-smokers. People who have given up smoking tend to become aggressively antismoking. They seem to be far more hostile to smoking than those who have never smoked. You would have thought that ex-smokers would be most tolerant of the habit in others. Instead, having performed a significant act in overcoming their smoking habit, their emotions and feelings fall in line. They now hate smoking.

Is there a useful general rule or life lesson to be learned here? You bet. If you don't like the way you feel toward someone or something, start acting the way you would act if you already felt the way you wished you would feel. Pretty soon, you will find your feelings falling in line.

For instance, suppose you had a major fight with your wife before leaving for work this morning. All day long you seethe with indignation at her attitude. All you can think about are the clever things you should have said during the morning's argument but were too angry to think of. Finally it is time to head for home, but you know the fight will resume as soon as you walk through the door. Wouldn't it be nice if the fight was resolved and your heart was filled with love and appreciation for your partner?

Remember the general rule: Act the way you would be acting if you already felt the way you wished you would feel. On the way home, stop at the florist and pick up a pretty bunch of flowers to take home. Is this hypocritical? No, it is merely acting inconsistently with your feelings. And acting differently from the way you feel is not only good; it is the basis of all civilized human intercourse. Not always telling people what you think of them is good inconsistency. Getting up in the morning for work although you feel like sleeping late is another good inconsistency. And acting kindly toward your wife and children even if you feel angry is also a good and useful inconsistency.

You are not doing this to change her or to make her forget the morning. You are doing it because it will help *you* to change *your* feelings. It will make it easier for you to overcome your anger and allow good feelings to displace any lingering hostility you still feel.

So you walk through the door clutching your briefcase along with your bundle of flowers. Your wife greets you with one of two possible reactions. Either she happily seizes this excuse to forget the morning's pain or she accepts the floral sacrifice and reminds you that there are still unfinished issues from this morning's argument. Either way, you are now in a much better position to restore marital harmony than had you walked into the house while you were still seething with resentment.

DEALING WITH UNREASONABLE COLLEAGUES

If you work with an unreasonable or unpleasant colleague, what are your choices? You cannot change his nature. You *can* quit your job, or try to get him fired, or change the way you feel about him. The last choice is the only practical one. This alternative will not necessarily convert him into a kind and benevolent friend, but it will cause you to feel less aggravated by him.

How do you generate warm feelings for a fellow worker about whom your only uncertainty is whether he is mad, evil, or both? The answer is KoRBaN—a sacrifice. You bring this unpleasant individual a gift. Actually, purchasing a gift for this monster probably feels more like a sacrifice than a gift. Is it inconsistent to purchase a gift for someone you detest? Of course it is, but it is also very wise if you are going to have to continue working with him. Giving him a gift accomplishes two valuable goals. First, you're going to enjoy the utter confusion he will experience upon receiving a gift from someone he knows not to be one of his biggest fans. Second, you will have deprived him of his ability to irritate you. You may never come to be truly fond of him, but neither will you ever detest someone to whom you have given a gift. You will have enormously improved your work environment.

This is the lesson of KoRBaN, the Hebrew word for sacrifice. You *can* change the way you feel about people.

CHAPTER FOUR

The Skill of Knowing

YaD-A

ידע

T those hygienically edited movies that airlines provide to anesthetize their passengers into compliant immobility just don't do it for me. Trying to be productive by opening a laptop computer is also out of the question. The traveler in front of me invariably reclines his seat back so far that if I yawn, my lower jaw will strike the top of his head and inflict a concussion. No wonder that on cross-country airplane trips, many of us resort to trying to talk with our seatmates: There is little else to do!

While earning my frequent-flier miles, I have participated in countless high altitude conversations and overheard many more. Invariably, it's a sort of dance to exchange information. Each tries to elicit from the other details that might include the line of work their fellow traveler is in, marital status, and/or reasons for travel. There are no nefarious motives; getting to know a stranger involves asking certain types of questions.

DO WE REALLY KNOW?

Have you ever wanted to scream, "I know, I know!" when some bore starts relating a tale you've already heard him tell three times? Or how about your child who, during an intense lecture from you about misbehavior, puts her hands over her little ears and says, "I know, Mommy, I know." Whenever we say "I know" do we really, *really,* know? Do we even know what we mean by the phrase "knowing something" or "knowing someone"? I think not. I suspect that many of us are not even certain of how to help others to know us.

Business, personal relationships, and acquiring inanimate objects are three areas in which we need to effectively use our ability to know. In your business and professional lives, you might want to get to know that employee before hiring him. You might need to get to know someone whom you are contemplating making a preferred vendor for your business. If you are applying for a job, it would be useful to get to know the company so you could determine whether you would really like to work there. And if you felt you knew that car salesman, wouldn't you feel a little more comfortable about signing the contract?

The second area in which we could all benefit from learning how to know someone is our personal lives. If you felt confident that you really knew the man your daughter was dating, you would be in a better position to offer guidance. Making new friends and keeping old ones surely depends on your ability to get to know people. Knowing the man behind the charming smile or the girl behind those sparkling eyes might help you decide if you really wanted to spend the rest of your life with that person. Similarly, continuing to know your parents as they change or your own children as they develop all require that you know how to know.

Finally, the third area in which we use our ability to know is with objects or facts. When I go shopping for a lawn mower, I try to get to know several machines in order to choose the one I prefer. I might study the highway code in order to "know the rules." My teenage son insists that he "knows" how to drive. I handle, try on, and examine the sweater that caught my eye in the department store to get to know whether it will suit me, and whether it is worth more to me than the twenty dollars in my pocket. I would like to know how to program my new video-cassette recorder to make it stop flashing green twelves.

Possessing the ability to accurately know things and people in different contexts seems to be an essential part of life. Just as in making an omelette, it is easiest when one knows how. Fortunately the Lord's language provides useful insights into this skill of knowing.

HAND AND EYE

The Hebrew word for *know* or *knowledge* is *YaD-A* and is made up of the three letters *yud, dalet, ayin.* The first two letters spell out the word for hand, *YaD.* The last letter, *ayin,* means an eye. *Hand* and *eye?* What do these two words have to do with knowing?

The word *know* is a composite of the two very organs that the human being uses to know—hand and eye. Could this be why, upon meeting someone for the first time, we give the person a firm handshake and look him in the eye? Coincidence? You be the judge.

The meaning of the compound Hebrew word, *hand-eye,* offers a way to understand what knowing really means. Let's start with the word *hand.*

If I were to call out the word *hand* to you, what might be the very first word to spring to your mind? *Fingers? Grasp? Grab?* Fingers only fold one way—toward the palm. They are the better to grasp and grab with. The beggar's outstretched hand silently says, "Give me." You may have responded to my little game with the word *fist.* That would have been fine, too. The purpose of a fist is also to further your gains and advance your own interests, just as grabbing and grasping are usually attempts to get what you want.

How might you gesture with your hand to someone who strolled into your office to offer you some jelly beans while you were on the telephone? Quite unconsciously you would hold up your free hand and mimic the gesture that traffic policemen use when they want drivers to halt their vehicles. Or you might extend your arm and point your fingers at the ceiling while showing your visitor your palm. The unspoken rule: Palm toward me and fingers pointing in my direction means "Give me," while rotating my wrist to signal the opposite gesture suggests "No, thank you."

Hebrew possesses the kind of astounding consistency one usually expects from a mathematical system rather than from a language. Perhaps that is because the Lord's language is both. You see, in Hebrew YaD means hand, or as we have seen, "give me." However, if we rotate the word and write the Hebrew word for hand backwards like this, DY, (pronounced *die*) we obtain the Hebrew word *enough* or *sufficient.* In other words, "No, thank you. I have sufficient." So we see that YaD backwards or DY means "No, do not give me anything. I have sufficient." YaD forward means a hand and suggests that I would like something from you.

Let's continue to probe. *Hand* is not the only human-organ word contained in the word *know.* The other, as we have seen, is *eye.* Is it possible that eye also suggests a similar focus on me and my own wants and desires just as hand does? Let's find out.

THE EYES HAVE IT

Have you ever bought something that later turned out to be unnecessary? I know I have done so more than once. Whenever I have impulsively purchased something, one of my organs is more to blame than any other. The guilty part of my anatomy is always my eyes. Think about it. Whenever your mother told you that your eyes were bigger than your tummy, she was observing the same thing. Somehow, the eyes have the capacity to powerfully influence our emotions, particularly those emotions having to do with our desires and wishes.

Marketers realize that if they want to make us act impulsively, they must appeal to our eyes. For this reason many shopping networks can be found on television. People will buy things they see on TV, not things they hear described on the radio. Those catalogs that fill our mailboxes are heavy on color photographs of the merchandise on sale. Most of us are not nearly as susceptible to auditory sales pitches as we are to the visual sales pitches of television, catalogs, and in-store displays.

Have you ever known a young man who fell in love with, and perhaps sadly even married, a completely unsuitable young woman? Often, when a man makes a stupid mistake about a woman, his eyes are chiefly to blame. Very few men abandon their wives and children to run off with women they have never actually seen. Phone conversations or computer e-mail might well have been the start in such instances, but full and final folly comes only when a man allows his eyes to dictate the rules.

I have often joked with single male listeners of my radio show, warning them that they should talk to single women only over the phone. No face-to-face meetings should be allowed. Men cannot be trusted with women once their eyes become part of the decision-making process. My advice is for them to get to know women only through lengthy phone conversations. This way they will avoid being sabotaged by their eyes. Some men become infatuated with unsuitable women because their eyes mislead them, while others refuse to get to know very suitable women for the very same reason: Their eyes mislead them. Eyes tend to supply very self-centered emotional data.

Now we might be making some progress toward understanding the true meaning of knowing. We have discovered that the Hebrew word for knowing, YaD-A, is made up of two words, *hand* and *eye,* and both imply self-centeredness. Hand suggests a tendency to grasp and grab, while our eyes seduce us into wanting things. What does this have to do with knowing? To further illustrate, let's watch people drift around the room at an imaginary cocktail party. The dance usually looks something like this: People approach other people, talk for a while, and then move on. As they chat, their eyes often rove around the room trying to find another, more interesting person. Conversations only get animated when two people focus on each other and stop seeking better prey.

You may have noticed that a party at which you only spend a few minutes conversing with dozens of people can be very depressing. In contrast, if there was someone there with whom you really connected, you may return home feeling energetic and revitalized. Only when you get to know someone do you have a satisfying experience.

What is the difference between the two encounters? In the first type, one or both participants quickly conclude that the other has little to offer, whether sparkling conversation, prospective friendship, or possible business connection. Both drift off to get to know other guests. In other words, both parties explore their new acquaintance from the perspective of what he or she might receive from them. How awful!

And what is more, that is pretty much how we all get to know car salesmen, friends, and lawn mowers. It is not really that awful either. Let me explain.

The Hebrew word for know informs us that when we get to know someone or something, we nearly always do so from a very personal point of view. In other words, we really aren't entirely objective. After meeting someone for the first time, we may say, "That is a most wonderful woman." In saying this, we are actually revealing as much about ourselves as we are about that woman. The point is that we find her to be a wonderful person. Others may not.

But the hand-eye theme in the Hebrew know tells us much more than that we are subjective in judgment. It also tells us that the criterion we subconsciously use when getting to know someone or something is: "What can he, she, or it do to enhance my life?"

WHAT CAN YOU DO TO ENHANCE MY LIFE?

It is well to bear this in mind the next time you are aware that someone else is in the process of getting to know you. In some way, the other person is evaluating what you can do to improve his life. Yes, I know that it seems as if it would be wonderful if self-centeredness played no role in human affairs, but it does. And it does have a very positive side.

For instance, the reason you can step outside your front door early each morning and reach down to pick up the morning newspaper is not because the paper carrier is filled with affection for you. You are able to enjoy this service only because the paper carrier is actually rather selfish. He delivers your morning paper because he wishes to be paid, not because he cares for you. What is important is that you are able to receive what you really want. Simply ask yourself which you would prefer: having your paper delivered sporadically and unreliably by a paper carrier who really loves you, or having the news delivered absolutely reliably by someone who does not even know you.

You only have to ask yourself which approach best lubricates communal interaction and allows a modern society to function: measuring the emotions others harbor within their hearts, or looking at their actions. As for me, I would rather be surrounded by fellow citizens who are all doing the right thing regardless of whatever naughty thoughts they were thinking, than by citizens who filled their minds with thoughts of love and goodwill but failed to act accordingly. We humans are not built for consistency; if it is to be a choice between bad thoughts and good actions or good thoughts and bad actions, I would much rather we all perform good actions and keep our evil ruminations to ourselves.

It is just fine if someone comes over to talk to me even though he is secretly motivated by finding out how knowing me might help him advance socially or professionally. If I were totally honest with myself, I might have to confess that in responding to his social overtures I am doing exactly the same thing. This is perhaps one reason many of us feel flattered and exhilarated to be invited to a party thrown by a wealthy and popular host. Part of us is saying, "Oh good, those people throwing the party are richer and more socially successful than we are, and perhaps being with them will allow some of that glitter and glamour to rub off."

Every interviewer talking to an applicant for a job is asking himself only one question: How would this candidate help me, my colleagues, or our company if he or she were hired? A girl deciding whether to accept an invitation for a date is likely asking herself how this guy might help her achieve her goal of being married and raising a family.

Paradoxically, by recognizing our self-interest in knowing others, we become aware of how we must behave for others to want to know us. Once we understand this principle, we ourselves become motivated to discover the ways in which we can do something for a new acquaintance. One of the important lessons adolescents learn when they enter the workforce is that their prospective employer is not interested in the fact that they are saving for a car. If they want the job, they must convince the interviewer that despite their tender age they have something to offer his company. And rather than babbling on about ourselves when we meet a new person, we should know that our new acquaintance also wants the satisfaction of speaking about himself. This is not a bad thing.

If we work hard enough, we will eventually reach the point with our spouse or other loved ones where we "know" them so well that their interests are totally intertwined with ours. Have you ever seen a mother wince when her toddler falls down and scrapes his knee? The mother literally felt the wound as if it were on her own body. A lovely story is related of a great rabbi in Jerusalem escorting his wife to the doctor when she was experiencing a pain in her leg. As they sat down in front of the medical professional, the rabbi spoke revealingly when he said, "Doctor, our leg hurts us." Can any of us ask for more than that from a marriage?

Let's return to the man engaging his seatmate in conversation on a cross-country airplane flight. When he asks "and what do you do?" or "and what field are you in?" he is subconsciously (or perhaps quite consciously) trying to discover whether there is mutually beneficial business they could do together. That is why these conversations typically lead quite quickly to the well-known ritual called the business card exchange. Rather than being predatory, this desire to "get something from the other" is the first step in developing human relationships. That is the secret of YaD-A, to know. We will all be more effective once we understand and accept both our own and other people's self-centeredness in getting to know one another.

CHAPTER FIVE

Reflections on the Laughter of a Baby

TZaCHok

צחק

As the father of seven children, I'm in a position to make observations about what people do when they meet a baby. Each time my wife, Susan, gave birth, I'd watch in fascination as family friends dropped by our house in Southern California to pay a visit and inspect the newest Lapin. If the baby was more than a few weeks old, the visitors invariably set to work trying to make my little daughter or son laugh—clucking her on the chin, laboring to tickle him, and so on. At times, otherwise articulate people sounded quite absurd: *"Koochee-koochee-koo! Koochee-koochee-koo! A-goo! A-goo! Boo-boo-boo-boo-boo-boo! Chucka-chucka-chucka!"*

After our guests departed, Susan and I would also have a go at getting a giggle, or at least a smile, from our precious newborn. And we would try whatever it took. For a mother or father, few experiences are more satisfying than the first time you hear your child laugh.

Getting an infant to laugh can be quite a challenge, as newborn babies have not developed the physiological mechanism necessary to produce laughter. But the desire among our visitors to win at least a smile was unquenchable. It was almost as if people were reluctant to recognize the new arrival as a real baby until they had heard it laugh. Or could they really be seeking validation of themselves by winning a response from the baby? Let's find out.

Why should that inaugural giggle be such a triumph for everyone concerned? A clue is contained in the first instance in the Hebrew Bible of the Hebrew word for *laughter, TZaCHoK.*

Contrary to what many of us learned as prepubescent Sunday school students, the Hebrew Bible is not a mere storybook or law code but rather a comprehensive instruction manual for achieving maximum human satisfaction and fulfillment. I usually think of the Torah as being the general theory of the totality of all existence. It doesn't *pre*scribe or *pro*scribe behavior and attitudes, but instead *de*scribes the sort of behavior and attitudes that are most conducive to lifelong happiness. Like any instruction manual, it defines its terms as it goes along.

When the Bible first presents us with the idea of laughter, it offers a definition of the term. One of the ways in which this is done is through the structure of the language itself.

"HE WILL LAUGH"

The three-letter Hebrew root meaning *to laugh, tzadde-chet-kuf,* first appears in the book of Genesis. There, the son of the patriarch Abraham and matriarch Sarah is born and given the name Isaac—in Hebrew, *Yitzchak,* or *yiTZ-CHaK,* literally "he will laugh"—as a tribute to the laughter induced by Isaac's birth. As Sarah says in naming the boy, "God has made laughter for me; everyone who hears will laugh with me" (Genesis 21:6). After all, Sarah was a ninety-year-old woman when Isaac was born, and there's something deeply amusing—joyfully out of kilter with the natural order of the world—about such an elderly lady giving birth.

From translations, you won't pick up something of key importance here but in the original language, just three verses later (21:9) the very same root appears, this time with a much darker meaning. Isaac had a half-brother, Ishmael, born to Abraham by the maidservant Hagar, and in verse 9 Sarah observes Ishmael doing something very naughty indeed. What did he do? The Bible is mysterious about the details. It does note that Sarah saw him being *meTZaCHeK.* Most English Bibles correctly attempt a negative connotation for the word and fumblingly translate it as "to mock" or "to sport," rather than its correct meaning, "to laugh." Thus, the translation reads, "Sarah saw the son of Hagar the Egyptian, whom she had borne to Abraham, laughing."

What exactly does this mean? Was the boy making funny faces or giggling at inappropriate moments? Drop your eye down just one more verse (21:10) and you will see that Sarah reacts to this by going nuclear. She insists that her husband expel Hagar and Ishmael into the desert, which Abraham, encouraged by God, proceeds to do. A bit of an overreaction on the part of Sarah, the mother of all monotheists, wouldn't you say?

That's precisely the question the Bible wants us to ask. Fortunately, Jewish oral tradition—conveyed in the Talmud and other rabbinic works and as old as the Bible itself—supplies an answer. The root *tzadde-chet-kuf* means "to laugh" but that meaning is only a spin-off, a secondary meaning derived from the primary one, which is harder to translate.

Basically, when one is miTZaCHeK he or she is acknowledging or committing a rupture of the natural, customary order of the universe. In other words, the heart of laughter is a violent contrast with the natural and proper order of things. The more violent, the funnier. In regard to the birth of Isaac, Sarah laughs in joy at the miraculous event of an old lady giving birth. There is something here that defies the expected course of events.

Most laughter we hear each day is in response to this general pattern. Take slapstick humor, for instance. What happens in a Three Stooges film when a dignified character like a judge or an ambassador slips on a banana peel and falls flat on his posterior? It's funny, right? It is hilarious only because it is not in the nature of a dignified, pompous individual to slip on a banana peel and wind up on his fanny on the sidewalk.

But what if you see a drunken hobo slip and fall? That's not nearly as funny, partly because we feel bad for the poor fellow, but also because it is indeed in the nature of drunken hobos to stumble to the ground. Again, puns make us laugh because a word is used differently from how we would expect. In successful jokes, the punch line delivers something totally unexpected; a joke falls flat when we can guess the ending. Laughter is one way of responding to something that conflicts with our expectations.

When the book of Genesis tells us that Ishmael was miTZaCHeK, it means that he was committing evils much greater than just making fun of his little brother. He was acting in a way that utterly violated the moral rules by which Abraham and Sarah lived. In that sense, I suppose you could say he was mocking his father and adopted mother. Without knowing this principle of laughter, we would have assumed he was merely engaging in boyish pranks and that Sarah's reaction verged on the insane or spiteful, which is unthinkable from the Bible's own viewpoint. But that is not what happened at all.

The traditional understanding of this episode, supplied by the midrash (an ancient compilation of rabbinic biblical transmissions), is that Sarah had spotted Ishmael committing the three cardinal sins: idol worship, immoral sexual behavior, and murder. So antithetical are these to a monotheistic worldview that only the strongest reaction was possible. As the first Jewish mother, Sarah realized the need to prevent her son from being exposed to the slightest indication that these crimes were normative. Any other sin might be pardoned, but not these, for they stand in direct opposition to God's order for humans. Therefore Sarah had to insist upon the expulsion of Ishmael from the family home.

And this, you ask incredulously, is the Bible's idea of humor? Of course not. TZaCHoK doesn't mean "humor" precisely. Instead, as I said earlier, the meaning is better described as an outrageous rupturing of fundamental norms. Such a rupture can be outrageously good or outrageously bad. Either way, what results is TZaCHoK, typically taking the form of laughter.

Virtually all forms of laughter spring from this violation of norms. When schoolboys furtively giggle about some bodily function or a sexual innuendo, their laughter reveals that, deep down, they understand these matters are meant to remain private. If those same jokes are moved from the suburban playground to the state penitentiary, we shouldn't be surprised if nobody laughs. Those comparatively innocent jokes just aren't funny to human beings for whom few rules apply. They laugh, when they do laugh, about things that violate their imprisoning world—matters that most of us wouldn't even find funny. That is also why there are categories of humor that are industry-specific and occupation-specific. There are jokes that only doctors find funny, for instance. This is because laypeople like us are unaware of the principles that the medical joke is violating.

IT'S ONLY HUMANS WHO LAUGH

To understand why a baby's first laugh is so precious, we must make one further observation. Laughing hyenas to the contrary, human beings are the only creatures on this planet who laugh. (Hyenas don't really laugh, of course. Their bark only *sounds* like laughter.) To be sure, dogs and other pets experience pleasure while eating or being petted. But they don't laugh. How could they? Laughter is a defining mark of humanity because only humans understand that there are norms in the universe. For that reason, we humans are the source of all laughter in the world.

When a baby is born, everyone coos and oohs and aahs and tells the parents what a beauty the child is. And to its mother, every baby is indescribably beautiful. To be honest, I must say that I consider most brand-new babies to be pretty funny looking. With their disproportionately large heads and rounded features they look more like Mickey Mouse than anything else. For the most part, all they do is eat, sleep, and defecate. Just think about it. If you are a new mother, you will surely resent me for saying this, but most newborns are limited in their range of activities to animalistic functions. When a baby laughs for the first time, long before he ever speaks, we are overjoyed, for the child has expressed a profoundly human uniqueness.

LAUGHTER AND GOD'S JUDGMENT

Not for nothing is laughter, TzaChoK, associated with the Jewish new-year festival, Rosh Hashanah. On that day, Jews believe that God sits in judgment over the world, portioning out the rewards and punishments as will occur in the coming year. That sounds pretty solemn, even scary, doesn't it? Actually, fear is not at all the mood of this festival, which is also called *Yom haDin*, the "Day of Judgment." On the contrary, we rejoice on Rosh Hashanah, a fact underlined by the biblical readings for the day, which include the story of Isaac's birth with all its accompanying merriment. The holiday is also distinguished by the repeated blowing of a ram's horn, a *shofar*, which interestingly enough is meant to sound both like laughter and crying.

In fact, both of these emotions serve as emotional releases, and both may result in tears running down the face. Surely I'm not the only parent to have dashed into the children's bedroom upon hearing wailing, only to find out that the noise was not crying but hysterical laughter. On the Day of Judgment, our highly imperfect lives are viewed in the light of God's very demanding expectations of us. The contrast between what we should be and what we are is so hilarious that Rosh Hashanah becomes the ultimate occasion for TzaCHoK, or laughter.

In that contrast, however, is our very salvation. Laughter makes us human. It affirms that we are not mere animals, but creatures of an all-knowing, all-loving deity. We are created by Him and thus given a supernatural, transcendent structure of normative values to guide us in life. But the Deity who gave us these rules by which to live also endowed us with the humanity that causes us to stumble and fail through the course of the year. Rosh Hashanah is a joyful holiday because we are aware that God, even when judging us, accepts our human failings and is eager for us to request another chance, another year of life in which to improve.

Without humor and laughter, it would be easy to overlook the contrast between what is and what should be. That would condemn us to spiritual stagnation—a terrible prospect!

It's not surprising that another function of laughter is to create among men and women a sense of commonality—of community and intimacy. As human beings, we yearn for and thrive upon connection with one another. Laughter binds us in our common humanity and distinguishes us from other creatures, most of which lack the gift of community. Just think how you feel when sharing a great laugh with others. Don't you feel a moment of genuine closeness?

Laughter joins people in all manner of ways, including some unexpected ones. One of the surprising ways in which laughter helps to bond people is actually alluded to in the spelling of our word for laughter: *tzadeh-chet-kuf*. In Hebrew, the letter *tzadeh* exhibits an intriguing relationship with another letter in the Hebrew alphabet, *shin*. This letter can be pronounced both like the sound *sh,* or also like our English letter *s.* The difference is merely a vowel issue. In the latter case, the same letter is not called "shin" but it is called "sin."

The general rule we must now visit is this: Conditions designated by words beginning with the letter *tzadeh* frequently lead to or bring about conditions designated by the word that otherwise exactly resembles this word except that they begin with the letter shin or sin. I think an example might help: In Hebrew, the word for *color* is *TZeVA,* spelled *tzadeh-bet-ayin.* Now replace the *tzadeh* with a *shin* and you get *SHeVA,* or "seven." Seeing the relationship here takes a moment's consideration.

Think of colors. Or better yet, think of the idea of color in general. What comes to mind? A particular color, perhaps your favorite color. Or more likely, the spectrum of colors: the rainbow. Now how many colors are in a rainbow? Check it out next time there's rain in your neighborhood against the background of a sunny sky. The sunlight striking the water produces a spectrum of precisely the seven colors that form the rainbow. Thus, contemplating color leads one to think of the seven colors of the rainbow. These connections are rooted in the Lord's language.

Needless to say, you won't find any such relationship between letters in English, or in any other tongue besides Hebrew. It is really rather remarkable. It would be like suggesting that English words that begin with a *p* typically designate conditions that lead to other words that sound the same but start with a *b.* As if by any logic at all, "patting" would lead to "batting," or "pumping" to "bumping." Looking in other languages for complex patterns of the kind one regularly detects in Hebrew is a hopeless time waster. But in Hebrew, profound lessons emerge from the exercise.

I said earlier that TZaCHoK has the ability to bond people in unexpected ways. One of the most profound ways in which people unite with one another is, of course, sexually. Sometimes Hebrew euphemistically refers to this form of bonding using the word *SeCHoK,* literally "playfulness" which, according to the last rule I mentioned, follows right after the word for laughter, TZaCHoK, on account of their respective first letters.

Does TZaCHoK lead to SeCHoK—laughter to sex? You bet it does. Just watch the local Don Juan attempting a seduction. Does he corner his quarry and beguile her with a learned discourse on the depressing thoughts of German philosophers like Schopenhauer and Hegel? Of course not. He intuitively knows he must make her giggle and laugh.

You see, biblical teaching doesn't limit itself to prohibiting incest or commanding Temple sacrifices. Actually, its counsel encompasses the whole range of human activity, including sex. And on that vital topic, we are notified that if you want to keep sex out of the picture—for instance, if a man happens to be dealing with a woman to whom he is not married—he'd better keep the discussion serious rather than humorous. Humor invites intimacy. Many well-known executives and politicians would have spent less time in the news had they recognized that playfulness with women helps lead to intimacy. Many a teenage girl has learned to her detriment that excessive joking with male friends has helped them to think of her in less respectful, even explicitly sexual, terms.

MAKE HER LAUGH!

On the positive side, when courting a woman, make her laugh! I remember advising a friend who had a long-standing but on-again-off-again relationship with a young woman. He could have married her years before, but he kept getting cold feet. Each time, he would terminate their relationship. Finally, at long last, the resolution to propose matrimony crystallized in his mind. He decided to act. It was a long shot, for the two of them hadn't spoken in almost ten months, but he wanted to burst into her life and sweep her off her feet forever.

My less-than-optimistic advice to him: Rather than make your avowal with some solemn declaration of love and devotion, do something loving but playful. In any event, engage her emotions; make her react to you with joy and laughter! When he reported back to me that his attempt at eliciting a giggle or a smile from her had failed, I knew that the girl was not going to accept him. Poor, indecisive lad. In the end, the joke was on him. But in a postscript I can tell you that he did eventually learn to laugh and to make others laugh. Today he is happily married.

LAUGHTER ALSO BRINGS GROUPS TOGETHER

Thus we see that TZaCHoK, in relationship to its derivative word SeCHoK, can bring individuals together. Similarly, the same concepts and principles can link groups together.

Few activities can as quickly enhance a group's sense of common bond as laughter. I generally don't enjoy art house movies, especially "artistic" comedies from overseas, which to me tend not to be very funny at all. But the art house audiences always intrigue me. I've sat through some painfully unamusing French farces, stony-faced myself, while the very cosmopolitan crowd of New Yorkers or Los Angelinos on all sides of me burst out in wild laughter every couple of minutes. If closely listened to, the laughter, however uproarious, lacked the subtle qualities you hear in genuine, unforced laughter. It just didn't sound *real*. And it wasn't: The movie wasn't funny enough to merit genuine laughter. But the crowd laughed anyway because, through laughter, the audience affirmed its place in a wide community: the community of people sophisticated enough to enjoy a worldly, cosmopolitan foreign language film at a New York art house theater.

These big-city sophisticates would be appalled to learn that they have a lot in common with us much humbler folk who enjoy TV sitcoms. For decades (though less so recently) sitcoms were punctuated by bursts of repetitive hilarity from obviously canned laugh tracks. Why didn't the producers of 1970s staples like *Happy Days* or *The Mary Tyler Moore Show* simply broadcast their shows and let home viewers supply all the laughs themselves? Because that's not the way we humans operate. We prefer to laugh in a community with other people who are also laughing. Sitting in our living rooms, we actually find a sitcom *funnier* if we hear other people laughing at the jokes. And we find ourselves more drawn to the show and later feel that we enjoyed it more. We felt more joined to other people by laughing together with others, even though their laughter was contrived by the producers. Laughter is so powerful a bonding agent that the artificiality of canned laughter barely diminishes its effectiveness.

Though all this may sound rather cynical or condescending, in fact, laughter joins people in other, much more noble contexts as well. Most of the greatest rabbis of the Talmud, for instance, were jovial. Before starting a *shiur,* a learned discourse on some legal or theological topic, it was a common custom first for the rabbis to make their audiences laugh. Learning is best done not in isolation from other people, but intimately bonded together with them. A good joke would get the learning off to a fine start. Great leaders like Churchill, Lincoln, and Reagan all had the ability to unify an audience through humor—not the harmful type that hurts and pushes people away from each other and God, but the positive, self-deprecating variety that binds people together through sharing an exclusively human experience—laughing together. And unlike the makers of French art house "comedies," these great communicators didn't have to strain for it.

As we've already observed, laughter depends on a structure of values that transcends our lives and gives them meaning. In the absence of such a structure, laughter fades and dies—which is why nihilistic, atheist regimes like that of the former Soviet Union have tended to be humorless. Without God to provide a structure as to what is right and wrong, we cannot be sure whether something is a departure from the norm. What was funny yesterday may land you in jail today. In contrast, genuine holy men are often found with a smile or a laugh on their lips. Beware of a person who wants to teach you about God but is always grim and humorless!

And should you ever find yourself doubting God, that He exists and that He loves us, the best proof that your doubts are unfounded is not the complicated theoretical proof in which theologians delight. It is the smile and laughter on the face of a newborn baby, and the joy it provokes in all who see it.

PART TWO

FAMILY

AND CHILDREN

CHAPTER SIX

Educated Hands

YeLeD

יֶלֶד

R abbi, my business partner has a son who is a patient in the West Los Angeles Medical Center. Do you think you might be able to visit him today?"

Although I did not want to sound heartless, my response to this type of request was usually negative. Being the rabbi of a large and busy congregation, I felt the members had a priority claim on my time. It simply was not possible to minister to those who were merely friends and associates of our members and maintain an adequate level of service to the members themselves. I wanted to ensure that people felt real benefits flowed to them from shouldering the burdens of synagogue membership. This I could best do by making certain services available only to those who had "paid their dues," as it were, by formally affiliating themselves with the community.

But the request to visit his partner's son on that busy Friday came from someone who was not only a member of my synagogue but also a respected and close friend. Fortunately I realized that this was not the time to be hostage to my own impersonal policy. Anthony was a Los Angeles investment manager and a leader in our community. He not only knew my policies in these matters, but he also had helped me formulate them several years earlier. Surely he had a good reason for his request. So I assured him I would visit young Roger Levin and headed out to my car.

As soon as Los Angeles traffic allowed, I found myself at the gleaming hospital tower and was directed to the patient's bedside. The first thing that struck me was how very thin Roger seemed. I guessed his age to be about twenty and found myself charmed by his eyes. They were bright and sparkling and appeared to have a permanent smile implanted in them.

I introduced myself, and to convert what might have become a slightly awkward exchange into a conversation, I asked him whether he knew that Hebrew was the Lord's language. It turned out that he did not know a great deal about his faith or its language, but he was inquisitive about what I meant.

"Well, to quote Sir William Bradford, second governor of the Plymouth colony, 'Hebrew is the language in which God spoke to the patriarchs of old,'" I explained. "More than merely a medium of communication between man and man, like most languages, Hebrew is also one of the means of transmission between God and man. It thus conceals within its structure many of the secrets that a benevolent deity wanted us to know."

His eyes brightened still more, and he asked for some examples, which I provided and which I later wrote down for this very volume. After we had grown comfortable with one another, Roger told me of the reason for his hospitalization.

It turned out that he suffered from a gastric problem that diminished his ability to eat and digest food. This malady was complicated by undiagnosed psychological and stress-related factors. He asked me what the Lord's language might reveal about his disease. I shared a few biblical insights, and we spoke for many hours.

Sooner than I wished, I could see the sun starting to set into the Pacific Ocean. This signaled the imminent arrival of the Sabbath, so I took my leave and rushed home.

I returned to Roger's bedside several times over the next few weeks. On each occasion we lost ourselves for hours as we meandered along the byways of the Hebrew language.

After his discharge from hospital, Roger became an active member of my congregation and experienced dramatic improvement in his medical condition. Now this in itself was not uncommon. Public health statistics tell us that people who are members of a religious group and enjoy close relationships with family and friends experience better health and more rapid recoveries. However, Roger's progress was even more exciting. He was soon completely healed and attributed most of his miraculous cure to something he learned from the Lord's language.

When I first met Roger he was pursuing a career in art, although his father enjoyed considerable success in the world of finance. He confessed to me that he had never felt passionate about art. He did not wake up each morning yearning to return to his creative endeavors. It became clear that despite being extremely close to his parents, he had embarked on an artistic career chiefly to make his own mark in a field different from that in which his father had achieved prominence. In this his parents had encouraged him, because they too felt that he ought to find his own area in which he could develop without being overshadowed by his father. It was then that his disease struck. The further Roger progressed in his artistic pursuits, the more debilitating his illness became.

JOINING THE FAMILY ENTERPRISE

Roger Levin's doctors finally ran out of treatments, and the only remaining medical option was serious surgery. The family consulted with me, and I recommended they try one rather radical idea before agreeing to a major operation: Roger would take a leave of absence from art school and join his father in the family finance business.

Roger's dad, Abraham Levin, was uneasy at this suggestion. He was reluctant to appear to be pushing his son into his business. He had always been disdainful of parents who try to relive their lives through their children's accomplishments and considered it a virtue for parents to encourage complete independence in their children. But in spite of his misgivings, Abraham confessed that he could really use the help of a trusted assistant and would certainly enjoy spending time with his son. I detected that he was considering the plan.

We have all seen parents who bully their sons into some preferred career or who nurture unrealistic ambitions for their daughters. In many cases, parents err by insensitively ignoring their child's true nature. And it is true that many parents force their children into roles that satisfy the parents' needs but do nothing to fulfill the latent talents and ambitions of the children. But it is equally true that many parents, fearing the accusation that they are trying to relive their lives through their children, drive their children away from a lifetime affiliation for which both parents and children really yearn. Many a family business has ended up on the auction block because the entrepreneur's children were unnecessarily discouraged from joining the family enterprise.

Abraham Levin agreed that there was little to lose by the experiment and invited Roger to join his business. On the surface, success seemed improbable. After all, what connection was there between art and business? How could a free-spirited artist who had been trained to respect spontaneous and sometimes unfocused

creativity adapt to a world of numbers and deadlines driven by very real consid-
erations of profit and loss? I recommended that Abraham and Roger view the
learning process as a father-son project. Pretty soon they started enjoying their
time together at the office, and Roger prospered as he caught on to the business.
Indeed, many of Abraham's clients preferred working with the sensitive young
man with the impish sense of humor rather than with his more driven and busi-
nesslike father.

Roger never went back to art school. He and Abraham later opened their own
boutique investment company, and Roger experienced a full recovery without
surgery.

What aspect of the Lord's language persuaded the Levins to try these changes?

Even as a child, Roger had always been devoted to his parents. When he
became an art student, it was largely because he sensed that this was what his parents wanted him to do. He was, unknowingly, acting out the meaning of the
Hebrew word for child, *YeLeD*. This word is made up of the two letters *Y* and *D*
with the letter *L* inserted between them. Now, the letters *YD* spell another Hebrew
word: hand. And the letter *L*, pronounced *lamed*, possesses its own meaning:
"teach/learn."

Placing this lamed (teach/learn) inside the word for hand, explains an essence
of the word *child*. In one way, a child is similar to a hand that has been programmed or taught what to do. In what way is a child an educated hand? The
hand is the organ we chiefly use to convey the things we either need or desire,
from the world to our body. Whether food, drink, book, or our paycheck, almost
everything we acquire comes to us through the agency of our hands.

Many of the phrases we use in English—as well as in many other tongues—
confirm our understanding of the hand as a symbol of reaching into the world
around us. These phrases include "hand it to me," "it came into my hands," "I have
the papers in hand," "lend me a hand," and "give him a handout."

AGENTS OF THE WORLD'S BENEFITS

Similarly, as our children grow, they too become agents through whom some of
the benefits of our world can reach us. One of these benefits, for instance, is that
our own social circles often expand as our children expand theirs. We meet their
schoolteachers; we often become friendly with the parents of their playmates; and
later we might encounter their workplace acquaintances. These new friends add
to our lives socially and, perhaps—if we end up doing business with them—even
economically.

During earlier times, nations and countries often found peace and prosperity by uniting with one another through the intermarriage of their royal families and aristocracies. Today, too, many families enhance the quality of their lives by the marriages entered into by their children. Happiness can come from these enlarged and extended families. Family gatherings for religious or national holidays, or family celebrations such as birthdays and anniversaries, are now large, boisterous, and joyful. When sad times strike, there are more loving family members to share the pain.

In earlier times parents often depended upon their grown children for their very lives. The unspoken social compact called upon parents to raise their children, while in return, during the parents' old age, those children would care for them. Back then it was perfectly clear that children were literally their parents' hands. The adult children did all that those original hands were now too weary to accomplish for themselves.

Today it is easy to mistakenly suppose that government-provided Social Security and private investments such as Individual Retirement Accounts render this old social compact obsolete. It may appear that we no longer have need for our children to ease our later years. Nothing could be further from the truth. No government Social Security check can provide the emotional gratification of children. No investment portfolio can offer the spontaneous surge of joy that older couples enjoy when their grandchildren bounce through the front door. What is more, those government checks do not come from some vast accumulation of wealth. They are paid, month by month, out of the paychecks that are earned by our children and by the children of our friends and fellow citizens.

And those investments of yours? What do you think might happen to the value of the underlying companies if our children suddenly ceased working for them, earning pay and purchasing their products? No, that old social compact is far from dead. It is alive and well. We still depend upon children in the twenty-first century as much as we did in the eighteenth. The next generation is most surely "our hands," helping provide our bodies and our very selves all those benefits that life offers and that we so ardently desire.

Not only do we see the link between child and hand through the Hebrew word for child, *YLD*, which really means "educated and programmed hand." Another link exists in the Lord's language that unites one of our limbs with our offspring. The Hebrew word for *sperm* or *seed* is *ZeRA*, and it is the word often used in the Hebrew Bible when referring to children. Interestingly, the word also means "arm" as in *ZeRoA*. You can see the words for arm and hand used in the same place when the Bible tells us, "The Lord thy God brought thee out of there (Egyp) with a mighty hand [YaD] and an outstretched arm [ZeRoA]." The three root letters, ZRA, of both arm and seed/children are identical. Once again the Lord's language clarifies that children and parents both benefit when the hand/arm metaphor is observed.

It always amazes me that many wealthy philanthropists create charitable foundations that they then staff with complete strangers. They frequently suffer aggravation while trying to educate total strangers about their values and charitable priorities. Meanwhile these complete strangers proceed to disburse their employer's wealth with which they were entrusted, often to causes hostile to the philanthropist's true beliefs. Appoint your own children, I urge them. Who is better equipped to intuitively know what you would think of a particular cause than a child whom you yourself raised?

YOUR ARMS AND YOUR HANDS

See your children as your arms and your hands. I recognize that this is not good advice for every parent and for every child. But it is worth at least considering. The cultural message that is beamed into our homes is that children must go their own way. Many will do just that, but many children will thrive if that cultural message is overturned. Many families will bloom if children are invited to become real hands and are raised in a way that prepares them for that role.

While growing children certainly want their parents to recognize them as independent people, they also enjoy being considered as "hands." Just watch how that little girl dresses herself in imitation of her mother's sense of fashion. See her beg to be allowed to help bake that cake. She wants to be seen as a member of the team. She wants to be linked to her mother. That is why she imitates her mom and loves to help her. Dads, if you are handy around the home, try giving your young son his own toolbox. Or better yet, earnestly enlist his assistance on some home maintenance project. Even though his help will undoubtedly complicate what may have been a simple task, invite him to participate with you. Be sure to ask for his help in a way that conveys your genuine need for "another hand." Do it right, and he will leap forward with unrestrained enthusiasm.

Should you be fortunate enough to own a family business, go ahead and feel free to invite your son or your daughter to join that business. Don't worry; if they don't wish to do so, they will decline. When inviting a child to become part of your enterprise, avoid sounding like a monarch bestowing a favor on a lucky serf. Nobody feels uplifted by receiving charity. Invite him into your business in the way someone with a paralyzed arm might beseech his limb back into service: "I need your help" is the magic phrase. That is exactly how Abraham Levin invited his son Roger into his business.

With the sun plunging toward the Pacific Ocean that Friday afternoon, I raced homeward to change for the Sabbath and to walk down to my synagogue on the Venice beachfront. During the evening service I noticed an elegant gentleman accompanied by a beautiful looking woman whom I had never seen in synagogue before. All of a sudden it dawned on me. Roger may have told his parents of our encounter in his hospital ward. In which case, they might have decided to attend Sabbath services in my synagogue in order to see just who their son had befriended. Following the conclusion of the worship service, I walked over to the striking-looking couple and took a chance: "Good evening, Mr. and Mrs. Levin and *Shabbat shalom* to you both."

"Good evening, Rabbi Lapin. Thank you for visiting our son today," they responded.

I explained that my wife would be delighted if they would join us for Sabbath dinner, an invitation they accepted. Today I often find myself thinking back to that long-ago Friday afternoon I spent with Roger in the hospital. It changed his life, but it also changed mine. Not only did it help teach me the power of the Lord's language, but it introduced me to some remarkable people. Roger and his parents all became close family friends. In fact, much later, when my wife and I needed some advice and help with one of our children, it was they who offered a *YaD,* a hand, to us.

CHAPTER SEVEN

A Place of Grace

SHuL-CHaN
שלחן

My bride and I had been married for only a few weeks when we decided the time had come to shop for some furniture. Maybe a mattress on the floor was sufficient for college students, but this rabbi intended to buy his young wife a real bedroom set.

"No!" my bride insisted. "If we are serious about building a home, there is another piece of furniture I would like us to buy first."

I was baffled, but only for a few moments before it struck me. Of course! A dining table! A *real* dining table, not that plastic-coated card table at which we had been sharing our meals since our wedding.

We began scouring the classified advertisements to find a secondhand, large, old-fashioned table. We shared a hearty contempt for the modern ones we saw in the showrooms. They all had long, thin, spindly legs and looked fragile, rather like a newborn colt. They were made of highly polished wood, clearly intended for show, and they looked sterile. We wanted a real table, one built to accommodate large groups eating hearty meals.

The two of us also shared an almost mystical conviction that inanimate objects could somehow acquire a kind of spiritual patina that reflects the use to which they are put. A table around which a family had enjoyed many years of warmhearted meals would surely reveal its history with, well, an almost happy kind of look.

Realtors often feel the same about this ability of things to reveal their history to sensitive people. They have told me of home-buying couples who would eagerly view a prospective new home. Occasionally, shortly after entering a perfectly delightful house, the wife—and it is nearly always the wife—will appear to lose interest. Inexperienced realtors will then try to lure the wife into the kitchen to try to reignite her enthusiasm. Invariably this strategy fails. More experienced realtors learn to live with this phenomenon. It is, they explain to me, the woman's intuition telling her that the house "just doesn't feel right," and this objection is quite impossible to overcome.

Yes, I am quite certain that most women and very sensitive men can often "feel" the problems and the pain that might have been experienced by earlier occupants of a home. In earlier days we might have spoken of the house feeling haunted. Conversely, some people can also feel the joy from earlier times radiating from the very walls and windows of a home.

So, my wife and I reasoned, if this was a factor with a home, then why not with a dining table? We wanted to acquire a table with a happy history.

We began each weekend by looking through the classifieds in the local newspaper. One Sunday we spotted an appealing ad, and after a quick phone call, we headed out to an address in Pasadena. As we were ushered into her lovely house by an elderly woman, we saw it—a very large, solid looking table made of great slabs of oak. There was nothing spindly about this table. It was solid and substantive.

The widow showing it to us was leaving the now-empty family home and moving to a small apartment. "There's no way they would be able to get this table through the front door of my new apartment," she confided.

My bride and I glanced at one another. Yes! We could both feel it! Holding our breaths, we asked the woman how long she had owned the table.

"Why, my late husband's parents gave it to us when we got married just after the war," she said. It turned out that she had raised seven children in that home. The one family ritual they had observed every evening was the family dinner around this very table. With that bit of information, we could hardly conceal our glee. We had found our table.

SUBJECTS, NOT OBJECTS

Why do we consider the time a family spends around the dining table more valuable and memorable than the same amount of time gathered around the television? One reason is that we humans find it much more fulfilling to be subjects rather than objects. We feel much more alive and more passionate when we are doing things, but we feel anesthetized by just having things done to us.

Don't you find it more exciting to paint pictures than to merely visit an art gallery? Isn't it more memorable to play a game than to simply watch one? Most of us would rather have a friendly conversation with someone than listen to a lecture, for in conversation we are active participants. As part of the audience at a lecture, we are passive. We are being acted upon, as it were.

Likewise, watching television is a passive experience. The television is acting upon us; we are actually doing very little other than allowing the tube to inform or entertain us. What is more, even if we watch television in a room filled with other people, it remains fundamentally a lonely experience. It is just you and the television. One of the reasons for the popularity of comedy is that the laughter links you with the others watching. It is a reminder that you are not alone.

Unlike watching television, however, enjoying a dinner with family and friends is both an active experience and a bonding experience. You participate, and you know you are not alone.

PLACE OF GRACE

The Hebrew word for table is *SHuL-CHaN*. Instead of the more common three-letter root, this particular word contains two two-letter roots and should be understood as *SHeL-CheN*. Here I remind you that in Hebrew, vowels are subservient in value to consonants and not terribly important at all.

What does SHeL-CheN mean? It literally means "of CheN" or "the place of CheN." Well, what does CheN mean, and why should my dinner table be its place? When the word CheN appears in the prayer book or the Bible it is usually translated as "grace."

Grace is one of those words we all use but would be hard pressed to define. Looking more closely, CheN is used in two instances: The first of these is when someone in the Bible camps or rests in one place for a while, and the second describes human interaction that generates economic creativity.

ECONOMIC CREATIVITY

How do these two apparently unrelated themes of staying camped for a while and creative economic interaction merge into one basic idea? Easy! Do you recall the meaning of the old expression "A rolling stone gathers no moss"? It means that someone who is always traveling will never be able to accumulate any assets. In order to create wealth, transactions must occur. And for economic creativity to take place, the participants must all be together in one place long enough to allow a transaction to occur.

For the most part, itinerant people find it difficult to earn a living. To be a sought-after employee, one must stop in one place long enough to acquire a reputation for skill and integrity and to allow word of those qualities to spread. Whenever we see transactions taking place, we should ask why buyer and seller bothered to stop long enough to effect the exchange.

Ask an airport shoeshine entrepreneur why he polishes travelers' shoes. He might reply, looking at you as if you were rather dull witted, "I do it in order to put food on my table." Reducing life to its basics, there is really no difference between his reasoning and that of the majority of the world's workers, whether they toil in the boardroom or in the fields. The "table" is the symbolic repository of the results of our economic exertions. In other words, a table really is "of CheN" or the place of CheN. A table is where we can see and enjoy the benefit of remaining in one place long enough to build the relationships that allow food to be placed on that table.

So linked is the table to economic creativity and prosperity that the Temple in Jerusalem contained a most important object—a table. Upon this table rested special loaves of bread. An old rabbinic tradition advised anyone desiring an increase in the ability to earn money to worship facing that table. This tradition reflects a true reality we can see today. Recent studies show that the one thing successful students have in common with one another is regular family meals. Not access to computers or great wealth, but simply regular meals with their families sitting around a table.

FAMILY STABILITY

I personally relate to this concept quite well since my own ability to return to work and put my shoulder to the wheel is enormously enhanced by the feeling of family unity, which follows our sharing a meal. My life is too hectic and the professional demands on me too high to guarantee a family meal together around our table each and every evening. However, come what may, each Sabbath my family does enjoy a particularly heartwarming Sabbath dinner together. The candlelight reflecting off the bright faces around our table always helps make me more emotionally ready for a week of hard work. Would it be too fanciful to suppose that an entire nation enjoys its greatest economic success if most of its producers enjoy similar family stability? If so, the dinner table is an appropriate metaphor for such family stability and perhaps the most potent tool for achieving it.

Do you remember your mother never allowing you to rush up to the dinner table and grab some food on the run? Didn't she always insist that you sit at the table until the end of the meal? In other words, she wanted you to "camp" or rest for a while at the table. Again we see the table, the SHuL-ChaN, as being the place where we should all stop, forget the clock for a while, and turn every meal into a little oasis in time.

Back when you were a child, you might have expressed youthful indignation at another of your mother's demands. Didn't she want you to wash your hands before coming to the table?

"Aw, Mom, my hands are already clean," was your cry.

"I don't care if they are clean, you still must always wash your hands before coming to the table," she answered. This served to further convince you that most adults were quite mad. This custom of washing hands before a meal came about because of a very ancient belief: Jewish tradition informs us that after the Jerusalem Temple was destroyed by the Romans about two millennia ago, the function of the holy altar was taken over by the dinner table in every home. In the same way that priests would ceremonially wash their hands before approaching the altar, today we all wash our hands before we approach the dinner table. To this very day, the Jewish way of preparing for the dinner table is to wash our hands in the same ceremonial manner as the priests of old. Rather than just holding our hands beneath the faucet, we use a special cup from which we pour water on to each hand. Many Jewish homes today are equipped with beautiful silver or copper cups made especially for this purpose.

You see, the dinner table, the SHul-ChaN, can and should be taken very seriously in any home in which family is important. The table serves as a kind of meeting place of the physical and the spiritual—or if you prefer, a meeting place of the animalistic and the divine. It is where we acknowledge that, yes, we eat just as animals eat, but we do so in a uniquely human way.

For instance, if your parents were anything like mine, whenever you made some dreadful noise they would respond by requesting that you kindly cease sounding like "an animal." To be told that you were behaving like an animal was a very serious indictment when I was growing up. Not that my family minded animals. In fact, just the opposite was true. We were frequent visitors of zoos and game reserves. It was simply that my parents knew that when people thought they were animals, things fell apart. By remembering that in crucial ways we are quite different from animals, members of a family can be expected to act toward one another with consideration and kindness—conduct mostly alien to the animal

world. On the other hand, if enough of us become convinced that we are basically
an advanced form of animal, then no reason exists for us not to do exactly as we
please, whenever and wherever we please, with whomever we please. People who
feel this way are usually tough to get along with.

THE MARK OF HUMAN REFINEMENT

Have you ever asked someone to tell you the first word that comes to mind as
soon as you say a word? Psychologists call this little game the association of ideas
test. Try it out with a few harmless trials. Say "pen" and most people will respond
"paper." Say "dog" and you will hear "cat." Now say "table"; most people will
immediately say "chair." This is another valuable contribution the dinner table
makes to a family. You have to sit at a table in order to most effectively use it.
Sitting is a uniquely human posture. When we recline, kneel, crouch, or lie, we
are doing something that animals also do. By sitting in a chair, however, we
assume a uniquely human attitude.

In this fashion we can again count on the dinner table to help maintain
human dignity. Instead of grabbing some nourishment on the run by opening a
can and gobbling its contents, we calmly sit down at a table. Though the simple
act of eating could be mistaken as merely an animal-like activity, when we sit to
eat at a table we are proclaiming our special humanness. To whom are we proclaiming it? Most importantly, to ourselves.

A PLACE FOR ENHANCED DISCUSSION

It is worth noting that somehow ideas seem more fertile and more exciting when
discussed at the dinner table. Thoughts flow more easily and people seem to listen more attentively during a shared meal than they do at a meeting, for instance.
When the ancient Greeks wanted to conduct a serious discussion, they called a
symposium. Even someone as serious as Plato would occasionally engage in a
symposium. Do you know what the word means? It means a drinking party. Yes,
that's right. The very best way to conduct a difficult discussion is around a dinner
table arranged with food and drink. Is it possible that you are more open to my
thoughts when you eat my food? Could this be why business professionals often
argue over who will pay for dinner? And could it be why, even in these egalitarian
days, most men on dinner dates still insist on picking up the restaurant check?

An interesting sidebar of world history illustrates this point. Many years ago,
a brilliant statesman pursued the dream of a European Economic Community. The
father of European unification, Jean Monet, wanted a building in which meetings

between nations could be held. He knew that this improbable project would take decades to bring to fruition. After all, Europe had been roiled by wars for centuries. One of those wars lasted a hundred years. Antagonism between France and Germany went back so far that nobody could even remember when they first fought. Sweden had contempt for Italy, and there were rifts between Spain and Portugal. The problem was how to get representatives of these sovereign nations into the same room, let alone forge an alliance into which each would have to submerge a little of his precious autonomy.

Monet's subordinates returned with photographs of some of the largest and most prestigious office towers in Paris. He gently explained that they had misunderstood him. He did not want a conspicuous, huge office building in the middle of the city. He wanted a quiet old mansion somewhere on the outskirts of town.

"Anything else?" his officials asked.

"Yes," he said. "The one thing my house will need is a great big dining room— a dining room capable of housing a great big old dining table." Responding to the startled looks on the faces of his associates, the statesman explained that any significant steps toward a modern family of nations in Europe would happen only around a dinner table. People are more agreeable while they are sharing a meal.

This is, of course, one reason for the business lunch. One would think that the office would be the best place to discuss a possible transaction. Yet, experienced business professionals know that deals work best at meals. This is just one more example of the magic of the dining table.

A PLACE TO GROW CLOSER

I may not be capable of advising the world how to achieve peace, but I do know that the overwhelming majority of young couples in whose marriages I have been involved share one important trait: Their acquaintance with one another ripened and their mutual affection grew chiefly during meals they enjoyed as guests in the homes of married couples. Perhaps the comfortable domesticity of their hosts penetrated to the very souls of the young men and women through the food they shared and the table at which they enjoyed that food. The terrifying prospect of marriage might have appeared to be a little less frightening and somewhat more inviting during those times around the dinner table.

A word of advice to those stalled in courtships that are not moving toward the altar as quickly as might be desired: Forget about those dates spent at a movie. Discard dates that involve you watching sports on television together. They accomplish very little. Instead, try this approach: Arrange to be invited, along with the object of your affection, for a meal at the home of a happily married couple you know. Repeat this treatment periodically.

If you know a young man and his beloved, you might consider helping them along the same road that has brought you happiness and fulfillment. Invite them over for dinner. Of course, courting couples should not be the only welcome guests. In nearly twenty years of marriage, I could probably count on the fingers of one hand the number of Sabbath meals my family has eaten with no guests at the table. I would estimate that, over the years, we have hosted a total of five thousand guests at our SHul-CHaN. Let me clarify. Do not, even for a moment, think that this hospitality is due to saintly, generous, and self-sacrificing motives. You're thinking of the wrong rabbi! Please don't even consider the possibility that we invite friends to join our dinner table in a selfless attempt to alleviate world hunger. No, we invite people to share our family meals because their presence and participation adds to the pleasure of our dining experience. Purchasing a large dining table as young newlyweds was one of the best ideas my beautiful bride ever had.

The look on the face of that charming old lady from whom my bride and I purchased our dining table revealed that she was just as insightful as the European statesman. With a wise smile she promised, "In years to come, that table will be the scene of some of your family's most meaningful and memorable moments, just as it was for my family." She was absolutely right!

CHAPTER EIGHT

Parents

HoRiM
הורים

Not wanting to look a gift horse in the mouth, I was delighted that Charla wanted to work as my secretary. For fear she might change her mind, I engaged her without probing as to why an obviously competent elementary school teacher was willing to come down a notch or two. It quickly became apparent that this was a stroke of good fortune for me.

As we got to know each other a little better over the next few years, Charla's story emerged. Having been trained as a teacher, she loved teaching the youngest grades. But eventually she had sadly concluded that within the school system there was little she could do for those in her charge.

What was the problem?

"Rabbi," she said, "into my classroom walked four- and five-year-old children who had never in their lives held a crayon, pencil, or book. They had never had an adult read them a bedtime story. They had spent the entirety of their short lives plopped in front of a TV, neglected by their drug-addicted mothers."

As a teacher responsible for a large class of children, there was simply too little that she could do for them. It broke her heart to watch little lives destroyed almost before they had begun. Charla decided that she could not spend her entire day surrounded by such tragedy; instead, she would volunteer to work with one child at a time. And so each day after she finished helping me with my work, she headed over to a church-run child-care center and tried to be a short-term mother to one child at a time.

Charla's story reminds me of a question that intrigues me: Why do some people emerge from hopelessness and destruction and build up their lives, while others become permanently crushed by the same desperate beginnings?

NATURE OR NURTURE?

I recall a story of how one girl, after suffering under the vicious Communist regime in Cambodia, was able to come to our country. Here she learned to live, laugh, and feel compassion for others despite the horrors of her childhood. How do we explain this? Why do some people emerge from dysfunctional families to become leaders of their generation, while a sibling may end up repeating the chaos of their parents' destructive lives? How can two siblings respond to adversity in two such different ways? What fills one immigrant with bitterness at rejection and causes him to turn to alcohol and crime, while another in exactly the same circumstances vows to make a success of his life and becomes a successful entrepreneur? American history provides us with a case in point. Think of the Adams family. Two presidents came from that bloodline, but so did alcoholics and wastrels.

Why are these questions so intriguing? I think it is for the same reason that stories of twins who were separated at birth and later reunited tend to fascinate us. We often discover that they share the most amazing similarities. Perhaps two sisters both married men named Frank, and each named her daughter Melissa. Two brothers find that they drink the same unusual beer, and both are known in their circle of friends for wearing a hat while everyone else wears baseball caps or goes bareheaded. Twins find that they drive the same car, dress similarly, and share food likes and dislikes, although they were brought up in totally different environments. What causes this? When scientists map out a DNA code, where exactly is the gene for Lexus ownership?

For parents, these questions are vital. Not because it matters whether my child prefers hamburgers to cottage cheese, but because I yearn to know if my actions and training will impact my son and daughters, or if they are preprogrammed in some mysterious way to be whatever they will be. It is a question about which learned academics and pompous professors argue constantly—the old "nature versus nurture" debate. Am I absolutely vital to my children's development, or did their personalities and characters come into the world with them? I recall that when I watched my first child being born, I desperately wanted to know the answer to this question.

NO SINGLE PARENTS

A glance at the Hebrew word for *parents* provides clues with which to solve the mystery. First, we should note that the word is a plural noun. Yes, there may well be many people whom fate thrusts into the unenviable role of single mother or single father. It is important, though, says the Lord's language, not to confuse that tough job with parenting. There are single mothers and single fathers, but there are no single parents. The Hebrew word doesn't acknowledge that this is a task that any one person can do. A single person can be a very good mother or father, but no single person can parent. That activity demands a man and a woman wedded into a unity and dedicated to the welfare of their children, either natural or adopted.

HoRiM, the Hebrew for "parents" (the *im* reflects the plural), is related to a number of other Hebrew words. The most important of these is *ToRah*, the comprehensive system of laws and codes that govern Jewish life. We also have the word *MoRim*, meaning "teachers." The relationship here seems obvious: Parents, teachers, and above all the Torah teach us how to live our lives.

But the word *parents, HoRiM,* is also related to another word. Its two connected meanings fill in a vital missing piece of the parents puzzle. You can see that *HoReH*—what the singular of parent would look like if it existed—is very close to the word *YoReh*. Although closely related to the idea of parenting, it can be translated as both an archer and the gentle first rains of the season that allow the newly planted seed to begin to grow. Is the Lord's language perhaps suggesting that in launching a child into life, parents are doing something similar to shooting an arrow? That perhaps our earliest instruction to our children resembles those early rains?

Unlike the English language, in Hebrew we never find one word standing for two completely unrelated things. If I say that I am buying sole so we can have fish for dinner and that the soles of my shoes are wearing away, you will be wasting your time looking for the common point in the two meanings of the word *sole.* Not so in Hebrew, where all words sharing root letters are related. So to understand what being a parent means, we need to understand the relationship between parenting and that particular type of rain, as well as its connection to shooting an arrow at a target. That is, the relationship between the word *HoRiM* and *YoReh.*

You will recall that early in the Bible God punishes Adam and Eve, and through them all of mankind, for disobeying His word about that tree. Adam is told that from now on he will eat only with *ETZaVon,* and the same word is used in telling Eve that she will have much ETZaVon in giving birth. What are they being told? A popular mistranslation of that word as "pain" caused some well-intentioned people to decry the use of anesthetic during childbirth as a violation of God's will that women should experience pain while giving birth.

Similarly, some translations mistakenly suggest that earning a living is intended to be a painful ordeal. The Hebrew text, however, does not say pain, but rather a very special type of "sorrow." What special type of sorrow could raising children and earning a living possibly share?

No Guarantees

The answer is that neither comes with any guarantee. And this can be very sorrowful. We all know people who put in hours of effort at their jobs, yet fail to see results. In spite of driving themselves relentlessly, the raises and promotions go to others. It does happen. Others work a lifetime only to lose all their assets in a stock market crash or through an act of war. There is no equation promising that if you put in an eight-hour day, five days a week, and are industrious and responsible, you will never be in need.

In exactly the same way, since the days of Adam and Eve, raising children comes with the constant worry that despite all our efforts, things can go wrong. It does happen.

This brings us back to the word *HoRiM*—parents. Much of what influences the kind of lives our children will live is beyond our control. Their looks, their intelligence, certain skills, and predilections as well as other areas are indeed implanted in them genetically. If they were little racehorses or big breeding bulls, there would be nothing left to add. Their destinies would be set. But they are not animals. They are little humans, and they are your children. They can overcome much of genetic predetermination. If both parents are below average height, that little guy is going to have to work ten times harder to succeed at basketball. It will be a challenge, but not impossible. If that tone-deaf little girl wants to become an orchestra conductor, she may be well advised to seek an alternative dream. But maybe not. I certainly don't know the limitations of her divine potential. A little boy built like a refrigerator who wants to become a ballet dancer? Well, who am I to determine his chances? He is a human with infinite capacity built into him. I'd say his chances depend mostly on the grit, determination, and confidence his parents instill in him.

Unforeseen incidents, unexpected opportunities, and unwanted setbacks will occur throughout children's lives and will affect how their lives turn out. But how they react to those events depends mostly on how good a job their parents did. How about those examples of siblings from the same parents who reacted so differently to adversity? That is partially, but only very partially, explained by genetic differences. In other words, the "early rains" fall equally upon all the seeds in the field. Why do some grow one way while others grow differently? Why do some plants grow red flowers while others grow yellow? Because they were different seeds to begin with.

But there is another far more important reason why different children in the same family grow up so differently. Which brings us to one of the most crucial and difficult challenges facing parents.

LEARNING THE RIGHT INSTINCTS

Parents tend to raise their children in much the same way that an assembly line worker adjusts a bolt on the chassis that rapidly glides by him. That is to say, parents tend to raise each child in their family in much the same way that they were raised. This is certainly not due to any laziness or indifference. It is just that raising children is such a full-time challenge that when some event occurs that calls for a parental response, that response must usually be instinctive. It is a bit like learning karate or judo. Why spend those long days practicing? Why not just take the book home and study the moves? Well, you know the answer. Events happen in rapid succession during combat. When your assailant grabs you by the throat, there is simply no time to quietly reflect upon the response recommended in your little karate study guide. By the time you recollect the appropriate chapter, events will have taken a turn for the worse. Well, raising children is a lot like combat. We become trained to react almost instinctively.

Most parents apply their instinctive responses in the same way to each of their children. That is a bad idea. One of the most difficult and most crucial challenges of parenting is to apply guidance in a way that is appropriate to the particular child in question. One sibling may need more flexibility while another may require swift and certain discipline. How incredibly demanding it is to restrain our instincts and carefully administer exactly the parenting that each particular child really needs. But how rewarding it is when one succeeds at this task. One reason parenting needs both a father and mother is that they can later "postmortem" each other's instinctive responses from earlier in the day, helping one another to gradually acquire the correct instinctive responses for each of their children.

Which brings us back to the rains and the arrows. Maybe the rain does fall equally upon each seed, but no archer shoots all his arrows identically. Different arrows may have different weights; may have different guiding feathers; may be intended for different targets; and wind conditions will be different for each shot. The wise archer handles each arrow in the unique way its mission demands.

Our role as parents is great. HoRiM serve as both the launching pad and the guide for their offspring, their arrows. Starting in pregnancy (which shares a Hebrew root with HoRiM as well), a mother can either sabotage the precious seed implanted in her, or she can nurture it gently and carefully. After the birth of their child, HoRiM—like the archer—can shoot powerfully and straight or, like the mothers of Charla's pupils, leave the arrow to dangle limply from the bow, most likely to fall to the ground.

We did not construct the arrows to our specifications. Nor can we control the winds that might set the arrow off course once it is shot. But it *is* within our power to do much with what we have been blessed. The fact remains that there is no guarantee. This should encourage us to turn in prayer to God every day. We have no choice but to acknowledge our dependence on Him to protect and guide our children. We can, to the best of our abilities, follow His guidebook and pray that the gentle rain will fall on fertile ground.

CHAPTER NINE

Twice As Many Sisters

ACH-ACHOT-BeN-BaT
בת־בן־אחות־אח

y son, Aryeh, occasionally—not more than ten times a day—complains that he has too many sisters. When a choice for a family video is put to the vote, he routinely loses. Movies based on Jane Austen books garner his six sisters' votes, while his lone dissenting voice gathers no support. And whenever there is heavy lifting to do, it falls on his shoulders.

To make matters worse, as Aryeh grew more proficient in Hebrew, he had a rude shock. As if six sisters weren't enough, the Hebrew language suggests that he actually has at least twelve. What do I mean?

Hebrew is an almost mathematical system of language, with reliable rules. Unlike English, it seldom baffles the eager student with exceptions to rules. Male gender nouns convert easily and reliably to female gender nouns by acquiring an *ah* sound as a suffix. Some examples might be *navi*, a prophet; *neviAH*, a prophetess; *par*, a bull; and *parAH*, a cow. Since the Hebrew word for *brother* is *ach*, one would expect the word for *sister* to be *achAH*. But it isn't. Rather than adding an *ah* sound, the word for sister is made by adding on the plural feminine ending, *ot*.

Based on Hebrew's grammatical rules, there is no such creature as one sister. Each one is actually a minimum of two. My son's nightmarish claim is correct; he does have twelve sisters—at least according to the Lord's language.

What possible lesson for my son, indeed for us all, might lurk here?

Living as part of a vibrant and vital family is joyful—not that it doesn't get frustrating at times. And not that it is without its burdens and limitations. It might be convenient if we were able to participate in family life when we felt like it and live alone when we preferred. But overall, since we cannot change our circumstances by the mood or by the hour, it is better to live as part of a family than in any other way. There can be little doubt that societies enjoy greater stability and prosperity when the prevailing model is the traditional family.

FIGURING OUT THE FAMILY

Families are surprisingly complicated organizations. Figuring out the family is a challenge, not just for graduate students of sociology but for every member of a family. Among the questions to ponder: Do children owe special respect to parents, as Judeo-Christian tradition demands, or should their main allegiance be to the state, as ordered by Nazi Europe and Stalinist Russia? What practical consequences could result from how we answer that question? Sticky issues are involved, such as whether children should be encouraged to inform schools about the lifestyle choices of their parents. There is the possibility that schools may feel justified inquiring whether children live in a cigarette-smoking environment. And educators might feel the need to know whether children are being exposed to creationist worldviews that could clash with the school's position on evolution.

Another question about family is this: Are husbands and wives bound by a holy covenant, or is marriage merely a convenient, and possibly demeaning, contract? The difference will determine whether children are raised with the idea that they, too, will one day marry.

Another question: Do siblings simply have a common set of parents, or is there a unique relationship uniting them? Should brothers and sisters view one another as merely members of the larger society, or do they owe one another a greater degree of loyalty than they do a stranger?

All of these questions need answers because how we feel about these matters will determine how we conduct ourselves in our family relationships.

For me personally, it is clear that family is a uniquely human form of social cooperation. I therefore consider it unlikely that families evolved accidentally or automatically. A more credible explanation for the existence of the family is that God presented the model as a gift to humanity. Naturally, those who are ideologically committed to a secular, materialistic view of the world will reject any explanation that includes a role for the Creator. They will need to identify an alternative explanation. But for those of us who are intellectually open to new ideas, the God-as-a-designer theory enjoys one important benefit: Our Designer was considerate enough to equip His product with an instruction manual. Furthermore, although the manual happens to be written in Hebrew, it is far more comprehensible than some of the instruction manuals that accompany contemporary gadgetry manufactured in the Far East.

Some of the profound questions about the family can best be explored by examining parts of this very special instruction manual. Before taking a look at the sister-brother bond, let us first glance at the other roles of children, namely their roles as sons and daughters. Here again, the Hebrew language departs from the expected grammatical convention in surprising and revealing ways. A son is a *ben*, which would lead us to expect that a daughter should be called a *benAH*. To our surprise, a daughter is referred to by a new word, a *bat* (pronounced to rhyme with hot). This suggests that the relationship between sons and daughters is quite different from that between, say, a bull and a cow. In other words, the grammatical departure indicates that a daughter is not merely a female son. She is a specific and unique creation.

Paradoxically, the more egalitarian our society has become, the more it has regressed in terms of its treatment of daughters. Visit the small villages of India, and to this very day, you will discover midwives who accept the equivalent of five dollars to murder female children directly after birth. While all civilized people express horror at this disdain for human life, India's sophisticated city dwellers feel much the same way about daughters. In cities such as Bombay, the government had to intervene because the country's richest and brightest were showing the same contempt for girls, using prenatal testing and abortion to ensure no female progeny.

SECULARISM'S CONTEMPT FOR DAUGHTERS

Don't for a moment think that *our* richest and brightest feel any differently. In the United States where for thirty years feminism has been bludgeoning us into renouncing our traditional respect for women, the same discriminatory assaults on females regularly take place. Gynecologists in America's most sophisticated centers have told me that they, too, see a disproportionate number of female fetuses being aborted. I would have to say that secularism breeds a genuine and dangerous contempt for daughters.

It seems that only the eternal wisdom of God, rather than the ephemeral ideas of man, is able to place equal value to both sons and daughters. They are both precious, but they are not the same. If a daughter is nothing but a female son, then she probably is indeed worth less to her parents. The Indian proverb would be right: "Raising a daughter is like watering someone else's field." After all, what will she ever do for your family? Your son may join you in your business, but your daughter will eventually become part of the family into which she marries.

The Lord's language puts a stop to this precipitous line of reasoning by showing us that a daughter is not just a female son. That is why the Hebrew word for *daughter* is not merely the feminine form of *son*. What a daughter does for a family is quite different from what a son does, and her role is every bit as necessary.

Societies in which sons enjoy prominence and daughters are devalued develop tribal cultures. A son absorbs his wife into his family, and since she doesn't count, her original family links are methodically obliterated. That society then becomes a collection of clans and tribes. It is only natural that struggles and conflicts erupt between these tribal families. However, with a Designer family structure, a daughter enjoys an authentically elevated status rather than the empty rhetoric of feminism. By retaining the spiritual links to her own family origins, she bonds the families rather than submerging her own identity into her husband's "tribe." She helps cement the social network of society into a seamless system that is not a primitive and blood-dependent cauldron of tension. Not surprisingly, in God's model, daughters are safer—and so is society.

In an amazing display of system integrity, the Hebrew words for brother and sister display similar patterns to son and daughter. The Hebrew word for sister is actually *ACHOT*, which literally means "sisters." (When intending to really say sisters, in the plural, the Lord's language contrives an entirely new word, *ACHAYOT*.) This is what worried my son. According to his correct understanding of this principle, no brother has only one sister. Even if Jack and Jill were the only children of the family, the Hebrew would indicate that Jack actually has two sisters. He would have to introduce Jill by saying, "I'd like you to meet my sisters, Jill."

TWO SEPARATE RELATIONSHIPS

My son felt placated once I explained that he doesn't *really* have twelve sisters. Instead, he has two separate relationships with each of his sisters: One relationship is with his sister, the single girl; the second relationship is the one he has with his sister after she marries. The relationship between a sister and her brother, or between two sisters, changes after a girl's marriage in a way that the relationship between two brothers does not. While he can count on her loyalty and devotion until her marriage, a brother would be wise to recognize that after his sister's marriage, her priority becomes her husband.

Similarly, parents interact with their daughters quite differently after they marry. The Hebrew word for son, *BeN*, is related to the concept of building, *BoNeH;* while the word for daughter, *BaT,* is related to *BaYiT,* or home. When he marries, a son's obligations to his new family "build" on top of those he already has to his parents and siblings. When a man marries, he is not leaving his family for another; he is bringing a new person, his bride, into his own family. However, as I explained a little earlier, he is to do so in a way that does not overwhelm his bride's personality. On the other hand, when a daughter marries, she is now chiefly committed to building her new "home."

I recently observed how a wise friend of mine, a great American, put these ideas into practice. He is an American of faith who served as a cabinet secretary to one of America's finest presidents; he has also built up a successful business. Once, while visiting him in his comfortable Park Avenue apartment, I commented how nice it must be for him to have his sons and sons-in-law working with him in his business. He quickly corrected me. Only his sons worked with him, not his sons-in-law.

Why not his sons-in-law? I wondered. My friend's answer revealed to me both the wisdom of the president who appointed him and the wisdom that president planned to gain by including this man in his administration. "While I am certain my sons-in-law would follow my directives as surely as do my sons," he said, "their wives—my daughters—would respect them just a bit less for being their father's employees."

This told me how clearly my friend understood the strange dynamics of daughters. His daughters, like other girls, need to transfer their emotional allegiance from their father to their husbands. This they could do only if they could respect their husbands as they did their father. Watching their father hurl directives at their husbands, in what was probably not always the most sensitive and patient tone of voice, could only make their task as wives more difficult.

He was hoping that several of his sons-in-law would join their own fathers in their successful family enterprises. This, he was quite certain, would be far better for his daughters' marriages.

TRANSFER OF EMOTIONAL ALLEGIANCE

When a woman marries, her relationship with her own family undergoes real change in a way that is not the same for men. Perhaps the widespread tradition of a girl taking the name of her new family reflects the fundamental truth that upon marriage, a woman breaks some subtle bond with her own family. While she certainly should retain very strong spiritual bonds with her own family, there ought to be a healthy transfer of some emotional allegiance. This can be hard for both her and her own original family. It is likely to be a difficult transition for any young wife, and it demands considerable sensitivity on the part of her husband. Done correctly, it leads to happy marriages as well as to retaining wonderfully joyful relationships with her parents and siblings.

As a father, this transfer of allegiance poses a real challenge for me as well as for the wise and gentle men I hope my daughters will marry. It will be necessary for me to help, rather than hinder, my six daughters as they begin the process of transferring their emotional allegiance from me to the new man in their lives. It will be necessary for me to begin to see them as new people, just as my son will have to get used to having completely new sisters. And their future husbands will have to understand that marrying a woman who enjoyed a very close relationship with her father is a great blessing. The emotional intensity of their earlier relationship with their father can be kept aflame in my daughters, but it will be redirected from me and toward their husbands.

Accomplishing this transfer will take most of the first year of marriage. It will also demand a sensitivity and maturity not always found in young men. But to marry such special young ladies, they will have to be pretty special themselves.

CHAPTER TEN

The Lessons of Generational Continuity

DOR

דּוֹר

I n modern America the idea of "apprenticeship" has fallen on hard times. I feel for a young friend of mine who works at a magazine. The publication's editors are more or less evenly divided between senior and junior editors. My friend tells me how the senior editors often reminisce about when they were juniors themselves and their own senior colleagues would take them under a wing and impart to them the secrets of successful editing and writing. Often, an older staffer would sit down with a younger one and carefully show him what he had done right and wrong. As a result, a warm personal relationship often developed between the two.

Nowadays, says my friend, this custom has gone by the wayside as old and young members of the editing staff go about their business independently. Intergenerational mentoring is a thing of the past.

Sadly, my friend's experience is typical. Whether in the workplace or the family, the importance of ensuring continuity from generation to generation lies behind the Hebrew word that means *generation: DOR*.

In Hebrew thought, a DOR is not a number of years, like twenty or twenty-five, but a measure of continuity on which all else depends. It is a spiritual, not biological, measurement. A child, his parent, and grandparent add up to three generations only if we can identify something beyond DNA that has passed down from grandparent to parent to child.

We can identify generations in nonfamilial contexts as well. Science, for instance, has developed all the wonderful innovations that make our lives easier and more productive only because information uncovered by one generation was carefully preserved and passed on to the generations that followed. That is why so many prominent scientists acknowledge their predecessors with phrases like "I wouldn't have succeeded had I not climbed up on to the shoulders of Newton."

A potential Einstein who appears on the scene as a young child, but from whom all knowledge of past discoveries in theoretical physics has been withheld, must start from scratch in his scientific inquiries. Under such conditions, he will never become the Einstein familiar to us as the greatest scientific genius of this past century. In fact, he'll be lucky if he reinvents the wheel. In one person's lifetime it simply is not possible to progress from the wheel to nuclear power without building on earlier discoveries.

YOU'RE EITHER GROWING OR SHRINKING

In fact, in the absence of such "DOR-to-DOR" continuity, we are confronted with something much more worrisome than a lack of progress: We actually regress. This is a very important general principle, and the magic of Hebrew alerts us to the prospect. We have to realize that we are either growing or shrinking. Stagnation is simply not a human option.

I remember one member of my synagogue who owned a small printing business. He proudly informed us that he avoided growth since he enjoyed his laid-back California lifestyle. Violating my rule of never offering unsolicited advice, I warned him of this rule we learn from the Hebrew word *DOR:* You grow or you shrink—the only option not available is to stay the way you are. It so happened that, just at that time, desktop publishing began to take off as computers proliferated. To remain competitive, most ambitious printers adapted and expanded their services. My congregant, however, firmly stuck to his guns, determined to keep his business at its comfortable size. As you can well imagine, it did not take long for his small company to become obsolete and irrelevant.

The rule also applies to personal development: We either move forward or backward. It also applies to relationships, including the most important one of all: marriage. We are either nurturing and growing our marriages, regardless of how long we've been married, or they are deteriorating.

Here is how we know this vital rule.

DOR is spelled *dalet-(vav)-resh.* I put the *vav* in parentheses because it serves as a vowel here, making it secondary in importance. As I have previously explained, when you reverse the spelling of a Hebrew word, important insights tend to emerge. In this case, *DOR* spelled backward is *resh-(vav)-dalet*. Dealing in consonants only, we are left with *resh-dalet,* or *ReyD,* which means "to decline." The operative principle here is that when you reverse a word's spelling you get either its opposite, or its negation—the state that occurs when the condition signified by the first word is absent. When continuity (DOR) is absent, the result is decline (ReyD).

My magazine editing friend confirmed for me what I already knew from reading his magazine over the years: It isn't as outstanding a publication as it was years ago. Oh, it's a perfectly fine magazine; but ReyD, decline, has definitely set in.

Each generation must be able to draw on the accumulated wisdom and experience of the previous generation. The giant international business consulting firm, Andersen Consulting, knows this. They maintain a vast central repository of information and experience, which has been gathered over the years by the thousands of consultants who have made up the company. No wisdom acquired by any of their associates is ever lost. They understand the principle of DOR, building each generation upon the shoulders of the previous generation.

CULTURAL CONTINUITY IS VITAL

This is one reason I worry about America. I fear not only for businesses that will suffer from stagnation if senior management fails to educate and initiate younger employees into the culture and traditions of the firm, but I also fear for American society as a whole. Do you recall long ago when our educational institutions regarded themselves as acting *in loco parentis*? They viewed their jobs in terms of acting as parental agents. Today our public schools and universities proudly denounce the past and "reconstruct" it. They act as if their mission is to drive a wedge instead of a bridge between each generation.

If you want your offspring to be your children instead of merely your biological progeny, the responsibility rests entirely upon you to ensure that this happens. This means doing such things as spending time with your children instead of allowing television to deaden family interaction. It means using time with children for meaningful conversation rather than merely tossing a ball around. I do not denigrate the time parents spend playing games with their children; play is valuable, but only as one component of an entire DOR program. Investing time in conversation is crucial. Discuss values, discuss ideas, discuss dreams. In this way you will help your children stand upon your shoulders for their own decisions and achievements.

In the value system of the Hebrew Bible, the responsibility of nurturing cultural continuity falls primarily on males. This is not a question of "ought"—in other words, I'm not saying men ought to be responsible for teaching values to youngsters. Instead, we are dealing with a question of "is." The Bible gives us timeless descriptions of how things *are*—what can work and what can't—not fussy prescriptions for how they *ought* to be. It is similar to the way Sir Isaac Newton described a force known as gravity. He did not *proscribe* gravity, he *described* it. An example of a proscriptive law is the speed limit on our nation's highways. If you violate that speed limit, you may get caught or you may get away with it. However, if you attempt to violate Newton's law of gravity by stepping out of the twentieth-floor window of a skyscraper, it is not a question of whether you will get caught. You will drop like a stone, and the sudden stop at the end of the fall could be problematic. Don't blame Sir Isaac Newton. He did not proscribe that rule. But he did describe how it works.

The Bible likewise describes rules built into the world by the Creator. Playing by the rules generally leads to a more fulfilling (not to mention safer) life than shaking a defiant fist at God. In our case, it is simply a fact that if males fail to provide continuity from DOR to DOR, generation to generation, probably no one will. Alarmingly high rates of single motherhood alert us to a society in which children have mothers but no fathers. In our inner cities we have already begun to taste of the ReyD-related chaos that this inevitably engenders.

Much that we count on in our lives depends upon continuity of training and knowledge. The benefits of thinking in DOR terms accrue not only to society but also to the individual. It goes without saying that my journalist friend would have been better off as a writer and editor if he had been able to secure a mentor. Less obvious is the observation that older professionals will take more satisfaction from their work when they can pass along their accumulated experience to some younger colleague. Being able to do so is a supremely joyful activity for a human. This is one reason we parents should feel grateful for our children, to whom we can pass on what we know.

If the history of religion teaches us anything, it's that humanity as a class possesses an ancient, enduring, ineradicable desire for immortality. No successful religion can do without such a promise. But there are two kinds of life after death. In one, the individual carries on as a disembodied spirit in a heavenly environment, which we mortals can hardly begin to imagine. In the other type of immortality, even after my death I can carry on my work, my dreams, and my visions right here on earth. How? By having played a role in training those who survive me. They become stand-ins for me. Through them, I can live forever.

But how does one go about successfully teaching the young? How do we influence anyone over whom we have some authority, whether they be children, students, or employees? The dual concept of DOR/ReyD offers a lesson.

STRUCTURE AND FLEXIBILITY

The key letters these words have in common are *resh,* which in Hebrew script is written ר, and *dalet,* which is written ד. Notice the similarity in shape. In Hebrew, even the appearance of a letter is worth noticing. In Jewish learning, these two letters, whenever used in contrasting words, immediately bring to mind another pair of words that also start respectively with dalet and resh. *Din* (first letter: dalet), is often translated as "law" or "structure"; and *rachamim* (first letter: resh), as "mercy" or "flexibility." In the spelling of our word *DOR,* the juxtaposition of dalet/din and resh/rachamim, in that order, yields a lesson in pedagogy: the science of teaching.

A good teacher begins with din—structure. Only when structure is established in his relationship with his students does he proceed to rachamim. To reverse the order is a grave mistake. As a newly arrived rabbi to Southern California during the 1970s, I accepted a position teaching mathematics and Talmud at a Jewish yeshiva high school for boys in Los Angeles. I asked the principal of the school, who had offered to walk me into my class on the first day of school, to let me introduce myself. (Unless General Douglas MacArthur, Winston Churchill, or some other awesomely authoritative personality is introducing you, it is sometimes best to introduce yourself. Doing otherwise can make you look smaller to those you are meeting.)

When I peeked through a window from the hallway, I saw what might have been labeled *Abandon all hope ye who enter here.* A virtual pogrom was going on. Boys were climbing over one another, shouting and shoving. Those who weren't engaged in unruly physical behavior hardly seemed prepared for the study of mathematics. On one side of the room a boy who looked as if he had recently escaped from a penitentiary was eating a sandwich. On the other side, another boy resembling a professional wrestler was peering out the window at passersby, while behind him a Frankenstein look-alike gazed dreamily off into space.

Taking a deep breath, I strode in and set down my briefcase. They ignored me. I stared grimly at the mob. My resolute stare was wasted—no one noticed. I turned my expression into a horrible scowl. It was as if I was invisible.

This was not an auspicious beginning.

I could see that this situation required a quick application of the first-din (law/structure)-then-rachamim (mercy/flexibility) principle. Now let me assure you that I am actually a fairly nice sort of guy, generally kind to little children and furry animals. So what I did next wasn't easy for me. Just necessary.

I walked resolutely out of the classroom, leaving the door ajar behind me so the boys could see what I was about to do. Just outside was a rickety bench, the old-fashioned kind with multicolored slats to sit on. I had noticed earlier that in the middle of this bench, one slat had broken in two and was hanging down to the ground. I grabbed one-half of the slat—a good four feet in length—and *rrrrripped* it from the bench. I then strode back determinedly into the classroom.

I now had the hoodlums' attention. Approaching the desk of one boy who was engaged in arm wrestling the pugilist behind him, I lifted the slat high above my head, took careful aim, and brought the wood down on his desk. *Slap!* As I intended, the slat struck the desk inches from the boy's hand. He looked up at me in horror and—yes—fear.

"*No!*" I exclaimed in an angry yell. "I missed! That has NEVER happened before."

At that moment not a boy in the room doubted that I was positively, dangerously insane. I growled, "This stick has a name. It is called Henry, and Henry isn't happy, and neither am I! If any of you tell your parents or the *rosh yeshiva* [school principal] what has just happened, or what's about to happen in the next forty-five minutes, this stick will hurt you very badly. Now listen to me..."

And I began to lay out the rules by which my class would operate. No boy would ever speak unless I recognized him. No boy would do anything in class except follow my instructions, concentrate, and breathe. Any violation would be met with swift and very painful punishment. I was fairly certain that I would be fired that afternoon. But somehow, nobody reported the details of my debut.

The school year went very smoothly after that. I never had to bring out Henry again. Those boys and I developed a real fondness for each other, and we were all sorry when second semester drew to a close. We had a fine time, but we also learned mathematics. After we have initiated a learning experience with a little bit of din—that tough, structured approach—we could then proceed in due course to the rachamim—the softer, gentler, more enjoyable side of teaching.

Of course, what I am offering here is an account of something I was fortunate to pull off. In the past thirty years society has taken a marked turn toward humorlessness, so you would be well advised not to go threatening people with a stick—even if you, like me, have no intention whatsoever of actually using it. But my point is that if we start out with rachamim, flexibility, the project of teaching young minds is often quite futile. Had I walked into the classroom and tried to sweetly reason with that mob on that first day, the rest of the year would have been an entire waste of time. Those boys never could have been induced to take me seriously.

The same principle may be applied in other areas of life. During the fifteen years that I was the rabbi of a synagogue on the boardwalk of Venice, California, I presided over some 150 weddings. My approach in dealing with newly engaged couples was consistent. Oh, they were often in love—making dove eyes at each other, sighing, grinning goofily. In each case I endeavored to pour a bucket of cold din on their heads, and Jewish religious practices made this easy. Marriage rites in my faith community are extremely legalistic, and include the reading aloud (in Aramaic) of an ancient text (the ketubah), which every Jewish male who wishes to get married must accept. In very unromantic terms it spells all his duties and obligations to his wife.

But this is just as it must be. First din—structure—and then and only then comes rachamim—flexibility. A marriage that begins with legalities—discussing the difficult issues, wrestling with deep questions that force the couple to articulate their worldviews—matures into a seasoned love that will last a lifetime. But a marriage that begins only with the emotionalism of love often ends in legalities. I'm glad to say that of those 150 marriages I shepherded to fruition, only three have ended in divorce. Future *dorot* (the plural of dor) will reap the benefits.

PART THREE

COMMUNITY

AND WORK

CHAPTER ELEVEN

The Challenge of Kindness

CHeSeD
חֶסֶד

There was a popular bumper sticker a few years ago that read, "Do a random act of kindness today." Obviously no one but Attila the Hun would oppose that idea. We all want to be thought of as kind people. We all would like to raise our children to be kind, and we want others to act with kindness toward us.

However, attempting to become kind is an enormous problem. Were I to tell my child to be prompt, the meaning is clear. I wish her to show up on time for that appointment and to finish all chores and assignments at the agreed upon time. If I want to be thought of as a cheerful person, I must stop complaining incessantly and begin greeting people with a smile on my lips. Attributes such as promptness and cheerfulness are easily defined.

But what exactly does being kind mean? Does it mean always yielding to the demands and requests of others? Should people trying to become kind and compassionate avoid accepting positions of responsibility in which they may have to discipline others? How much of one's income should be donated in order to fulfill the requirements of kindness and compassion? This is the problem with kindness. It sounds nice in principle until one attempts to define it.

Years ago a member of my synagogue who worked as a pediatric nurse told me about a young mother who brought her infant in for the baby's first immunizations.

As the doctor picked up the syringe, the mother began sobbing, grabbed her baby, and fled the room saying, "It's going to be too painful." While some parents are rightfully wary of immunizations because of potential side effects, this mother was not making a reasoned and thoughtful decision. She was reacting emotionally and, in her view, with compassion. My guess is that she thought of herself as an extremely kind person, perhaps one who avoided stepping on ants and never passed a beggar without dropping a coin in his lap. Yet, as any parent who is aware of the crippling effect of some dangerous childhood diseases could tell you, she may actually have been acting with great cruelty. She was putting her own emotions ahead of her child's real needs.

In the same way, a teacher who is too kind to fail a lazy student may be setting that child up for a life of failure. A judge who lets a first-time adolescent offender off too easily runs the risk of the youth interpreting that kindness as license to become even more brazen and ruthless in the future.

Dispensing money indiscriminately to people can have the opposite of the intended effect. All too often, the apparently kind action of giving someone money backfires and ends up in waste or harm. Oprah Winfrey generously donated vast sums of money toward a housing project for poor people. She finally conceded defeat and withdrew her support of the project when the housing was destroyed by those it was intended to benefit.

GENUINE KINDNESS IS ALWAYS LINKED TO GOD

So how are we to know if we are truly being kind?

The Hebrew word for an act of profound kindness is *CHeSeD*. Interestingly, God Himself commits both the first and last acts of CheSeD chronicled in the Hebrew Bible. He tailors suits of clothing for Adam and Eve after their fig leaves proved inadequate. Helping people clothe themselves in a dignified fashion is considered to be a greater act of kindness, CHeSeD, than giving them food. This is because the latter alleviates only a physical discomfort while clothing protects human dignity.

Doing someone a kindness while expecting no repayment is also seen as a special act of CHeSeD. At the close of the book of Deuteronomy, God buries Moses. Burying someone is an act of kindness that the recipient will never be able to repay. Thus, God's own book, the Torah, opens and closes with the Creator modeling true kindness, or CHeSeD.

The important message for us is that kindness can only be defined by reference to God and His rules. Aha! Here we have the faintest hint of a solution to our dilemma. Somehow genuine kindness must be linked to God. Attempts at secular or atheistically based kindness might be doomed by the absence of any defining framework. Let us see just how closely kindness is linked to the Lord.

Even the English language reveals the connection between God and acts of kindness. As Indo-European languages gradually evolved out of Hebrew, one of the challenges was how to deal with Hebrew's guttural *ch* sound. That letter *chet,* the eighth of the Hebrew alphabet, is used to open the word *CHanuka,* for instance. Most Americans pronounce the name of that holiday as if it were written *Hanuka.* Yet the letter *chet* is actually intended to be a guttural, back-of-the-throat, growl-like sound.

Several European languages such as Dutch and German retained that guttural sound for their letter *G.* Traces of this remain in English to this very day. For example, there is no logical reason why the written form of the number that follows seven should not be written *ate.* That gutteral growl of a *gh* in the middle of the word *eight* is only there because of the word's original link to Hebrew's eighth letter, chet. You can see both the *ch* and the *t* sounds of the word *eight* in that Hebrew letter chet.

The Greek alphabet starts off with *alpha, beta, gamma,* because it is based upon the Hebrew alphabet, whose first three letters are *aleph, bet,* and *gimmel.* Or, if you prefer, *A, B, G.* Only later did they lop off the tail of the *G* to make a softer *g* sound, namely the *C* as in *tic,* which we use in English. Thus with *C* being an heir of the *G,* we can see that CH or GH are essentially the same sound in the early phases of European language development.

This means that if we transliterate the Hebrew word for kindness, CHeSeD, into English, instead of using the two letters *C* and *H* together to represent the first syllable—the single Hebrew letter *chet*—we could use GH, which in English at the beginning of a word is pronounced *g* as in *ghetto.* This lets us transliterate CHeSed as G-S-D. You can see that we are getting quite close to G-O-D. It is a bit like a detective story or an archaeological dig.

Let's look more closely at the middle letter of the trio, *S.* Glance at the sequence of letters in the Hebrew alphabet starting from the eleventh letter, *Kaf.* We find the sequence to be *kaf, lamed, mem, nun,* and *samech.* If we write the sounds of each letter it looks like this: K, L, M, N, S. Notice how the English alphabet grew directly from these seeds: K, L, M, N, O.

How did samech with its *S* sound evolve into *O?* If we can resolve this problem, it will be clearer to us just how the Hebrew word expressing the ultimate in kindness became the very word we all use for the Creator, the origin of all our understanding of kindness—God.

Examine the Hebrew letter samech. This is what it looks like in Hebrew: O. See, a nice round circle. Interestingly enough, each letter in the Hebrew alphabet has an intrinsic connection to the first time it appears at the start of a word in the Bible. The first use of the letter samech at all in the Bible is as the initial letter of the word *encircle*. Although every other letter in the Hebrew alphabet occurs by the sixteenth verse of the Bible, this letter alone lingers unused for some forty verses after it finally makes its significant appearance in the very word that expresses its shape. Coincidence? Of course not.

Greek originally evolved out of the Semitic languages, most notably Hebrew. The Greek letter that was pronounced as a long O sound (as in home), was the letter *omega*. If we replace the O with an S we can make out the Hebrew letter *samech*. (The consonants in omega once we switch the O for an S look like this: *SoMeGa* or *SaMeCH*.) One can readily imagine a round letter that resembles a human mouth saying *oh* evolving into the sound one gets by doing exactly that. Whether that happened in the Greek period or during some other time in history is not important. The main point is that our word for the Almighty, the word *GOD*, or to go back a step the German word *Gott*, clearly and appropriately originated in the Hebrew *G-S-D* word for ultimate kindness.

The Oxford English Dictionary correctly identifies the meaning of the word *good-bye* as "God be with you." Thus we can deduce that the English word *good* derives directly from the source of all good, God. You can see where I am going here. Not only is there a logical argument to be made that all attempts to define goodness or kindness without a frame of reference are doomed; there is also a compelling linguistic argument that originally, humans understood that God and kindness were not two separate ideas. They were not even two separate words. For as long as they were understood as a sort of merged reality, each dependent upon the other for its meaning, mankind was better off. However, once a culture commences to define kindness with a political frame of reference instead of a religious one, it might be stepping on to the slippery slope that ultimately converts kindness to cruelty and tyranny.

By way of reassuring the skeptical reader, here are other indications that the original Hebrew letter S gradually became an O in popular usage. If our hypothesis of the Hebrew letter S and English O switcheroo is in fact correct, surely we would expect to find other instances of words that contain an S in Hebrew but an O in English. Right?

Sure enough, we have any number of such words. Many people are familiar with the Passover observance of the *SeDeR*, that celebratory meal reliving the

Exodus from Egypt. Ask anyone familiar with basic Hebrew what the word *SeDeR* means, and he will tell you that SeDeR means *OrDeR*, which is why the meal is conducted according to a printed agenda called a *Hagada* depicting the order of the meal.

Did you notice the transposition of *O* for *S*? The *S* in Hebrew's SeDeR became the *O* in English's OrDeR. Terrific!

There are of course many other examples of that Hebrew *S* sound becoming an English *O* sound. For instance, the English word *omen* derives from the Hebrew word for an omen or a sign, which is *SiMeN*. Remembering that vowel sounds in Hebrew are subsidiary and changeable, we can see that the three root letters of O-MeN resemble the original Hebrew word Si-MeN.

KINDNESS WITHOUT GOD DOES NOT WORK

Why is it so appropriate that our language should reflect God as the source of all kindness? After all, He certainly possesses vital attributes other than kindness, such as being omnipresent or all-powerful, that could just as appropriately have been the source of His name, God. The answer is that of all God's qualities, kindness alone lends itself to confusion. The message being sent to us through the Hebrew language is that kindness, as an attribute independent of God, doesn't really work.

Individuals who don't believe in God may indeed be kind, but a society cannot survive unless there is an unchangeable, immutable definition of right and wrong. Civilization as we know it cannot last if during one generation murdering old folk or unborn children is wrong, but twenty years later euthanasia and abortion are preached as the kindest way to deal with people who have a less than perfect "quality of life."

Parents and teachers need to know that their role is to guide and mold those in their care in God's ways. By definition they will be treating their charges kindly. Earlier generations were more aware of this unbreakable link between God and goodness, how the former firmly defined the latter. Those who now forget that link are unintentionally leading us back toward a primitive barbarism, all the while proclaiming a great commitment to kindness and compassion.

As parents, community leaders, and professionals we should always remain vigilant against the tyranny of kindness and compassion without God. Without Him, those words mean, as Alice in Wonderland would understand, exactly what we want them to mean, neither more nor less.

CHAPTER TWELVE

Settling Disputes

ChoLeK
חלק

The following scenario will be familiar to any parent.

Johnny and Sally are squabbling over the single remaining orange nestled innocently in the fruit basket. Both tykes are ready to do battle rather than yield to the other. This incessant sibling rivalry is threatening to drive Mom mad! What she really wants to do is seize the orange and hurl it across the yard safely out of reach of either child. Fortunately, she's enough in control of herself to recognize that such an angry reaction would be just as childish as the misbehavior of the two pint-sized adversaries presently glaring at one another. With exaggerated calm, Mom starts talking through gritted teeth.

"Why do you want the orange, Johnny? What do you want to do with it?" Johnny reacts with indignation. He has been playing ball in the hot sun. He is thirsty. He intends to use Mom's new electric squeezer (which fascinates him) to extract some refreshing orange juice.

Sally erupts in fury. "No, he can't do that. I want that orange!"

"And what are you going to do with the orange, Sally?" inquires a mother beginning to regain her composure. Well, guess what? Sally is baking her first-ever from-scratch cake. No more cake mixtures for her; she is old enough to follow a recipe. And this recipe calls for grated orange rind!

With a sigh of relief, Mom launches a lesson in cooperation. "It always pays to talk things through with people before starting a fight," she explains. Just a short conversation has revealed that both children can obtain their objectives from the single orange: Johnny can have his orange juice, and Sally can have her grated orange rind.

This little tale is more relevant to daily life than we might imagine.

It is in the nature of people to squabble. Most of us can think of many more things we want than we have the ability to obtain. Happy living sometimes involves restraining those rather vague wants and desires from turning into appetites and obsessions. If someone else takes hold of something we not only want, but perhaps even consider to be our "right," we have the makings of a squabble. There are thousands of ways in which well-intentioned people can disagree with one another over property. This is human nature. Otherwise, why would so much of the Torah consist of rules for settling property disagreements?

CIVILIZED DISPUTE SETTLEMENT

This is why every civilized society possesses a legal system to settle such disagreements in a civilized fashion. We do not aim for a society with no disagreements; that would be unrealistic. Spending time trying to build such a utopia would also deflect our attention from what we really could accomplish, which is a fair and just system for settling inevitable disputes.

In olden times and in remote lands, savages would club one another to death. These days we more often resort to lawsuits. "See you in court" has become today's relatively civilized version of the Wild West's showdown. With more lawyers in Los Angeles than in all of Japan, we have probably become overlitigious, but that is still better than the law of the jungle which prevails in many other countries to this day.

Part of growing up is getting to the point where we understand that we seldom get everything we want. Sometimes we just wisely accept that fact and devote our energies to productive enterprises. Other times we decide that an argument is necessary. However not every argument requires that one party win and the other lose. Although we may not always get everything we want, in many instances we can achieve our main objective while allowing the other party to do the same. This can be done without resorting to courtrooms or even to an adversarial disagreement.

Today in increasing numbers litigants are resorting to a process called mediation, in which they work with a mediator who plays the role of Mom. The mediator helps them locate areas of agreement and assists in the process of helping both sides win. If the process fails, they can then resort to an adversarial courtroom encounter.

The Hebrew verb meaning "to argue" reflects this reality. It is based on the word *ChoLeK*, which literally means an element or component. This implies that when one person is arguing with another, quite naturally, he expresses the one component or element of the debate that most closely advocates his own position. As listeners we have to remember that what we are hearing is only part of the entire story. Any responsible judge knows that he should not reach a decision until he has listened to both sides. Until that happens he has only heard part of the story. This seems almost self-evident; however, it is really counterintuitive. We may know better, but our intuitive reaction to a disagreement that involves us is to assume that our own viewpoint is right and the other is wrong. Our own position sounds more reasonable and logical. Anyone failing to fall into line with our outlook is in our view an obtuse fool.

In almost every disagreement in which we find ourselves it is worthwhile to remember these two principles: Each side is utterly persuaded of the justice of his cause, and each side is utterly persuaded that if he does not win, he will lose. In many cases we would gain much by at least considering the possibility that these two assumptions are wrong. We should at least suspect that the two positions may in fact be complementary and that all we have to do is find the key to the puzzle.

MERGING INCOMPATIBLE VIEWS

The puzzle, of course, is how to merge two apparently incompatible views into one synthesized entity. Fortunately an exercise exists that helps mediate disputes.

You see, before we can effectively mediate external conflicts, we have to improve our abilities to cope with internal contradictions. We all instinctively yearn for clarity and simplicity in our lives. We tend to prefer things in black-and-white. For instance, the phrase "You can't both be right" springs easily to our lips, but the real world is quite different. To avoid and resolve conflict, it is indeed essential to be able to hold contradictory ideas comfortably in our minds.

I had to teach this lesson to a member of my synagogue when he called to tell me that his father had just died. This is nearly always one of the most traumatic ordeals any man will endure. In his particular case it was additionally complicated by the fact that he was the sole heir to his late father's stupendous wealth. When we met an hour later, my friend was in anguish. He had been tormenting himself, trying to overwhelm his being with what he considered an appropriate sensation of grief. However, he also was struggling with an unwelcome urge to break into hysterical laughter at the thought of never having to worry about money again. He was confused and miserable at the guilt he felt about not being able to concentrate exclusively on sadness.

Once I had explained that God intended humans to be able to function with two contradictory thoughts and feelings simultaneously, my friend felt much better. It was for this reason, I told him, that the Bible informs us what sort of cargo was being transported by the Arab traders who bought Joseph from his brothers. Who cares that they were carrying fragrant spices? A young boy had been seized from the bosom of his family and would never see his beloved father again. He was bound and a reluctant part of a caravan of traders. The lesson is that even under these anxious conditions, Joseph enjoyed being surrounded by the aromatic perfumes that accompanied him on his journey to anticipated slavery.

ONLY GOD CAN PERFORM TWO ACTIONS AT A TIME

Although we must certainly develop our abilities to function comfortably while thinking contradictory thoughts, humans are restricted to only one action at a time. It was fine for my congregant to think and feel both joy and sadness at the same time. However, during the funeral and the subsequent week of mourning he was to confine his actions to those appropriate to mourning.

Ancient Jewish wisdom turns to the Bible to demonstrate another facet of this principle. The Bible presents two separate versions of the fourth commandment, which concerns the Sabbath day. In Exodus 20:8 we can read, "*Remember* the sabbath day, to keep it holy." Later, in the last of the Five Books of Moses where the Ten Commandments are repeated, the fourth commandment reads, "*Guard* the Sabbath Day to keep it holy" (Deuteronomy 5:12, The Jerusalem Bible). Well, which was it? Did God say "remember" or did He say "guard"? Surely it had to be one or the other.

There is a school of biblical criticism that I utterly reject as frivolous, dishonest, and anti-intellectual. Nonetheless, this school of thought has long insisted that a succession of different humans authored the Torah. They talk of a series of documents identified by letters, such as the J document, or the E document. This so-called Documentary Hypothesis serves mostly to reveal the academics' lack of familiarity with the Hebrew language and all its literature. Furthermore, these academics describe how some rather incompetent editor "redacted" or assembled all these old accounts into the one book we today call the Bible.

There are many reasons why I know they are mistaken. One reason is that they cite these two slightly different versions of the Ten Commandments, one in

Exodus and one in Deuteronomy, as evidence for the existence of several discon-nected biblical accounts. For one thing, this presumed editor, for whose existence no evidence can be found, must have been a little slow on the uptake to have not noticed the difference between *remember* and *guard*. On the other hand, if he did notice the variation in accounts, was not his job to edit the different accounts into one integrated volume? Why didn't he simply determine whether to use *remember* or *guard* and thus settle the matter for all time? At the very least, having decided apparently to leave both words in place in spite of the conflict, he should have left us a note explaining his reasoning.

He neither resolved nor explained the conflict because he never existed. The two conflicting words, *remember* and *guard,* were in the fourth commandment from that original day at Mount Sinai. The ancient Israelites would never have tampered with the holy text, and they had no desire to since their oral tradition fully and satisfactorily explained the purpose for these two versions of the fourth commandment. This oral tradition teaches that God, in a way that obviously only He could, indeed spoke both words simultaneously. For human ears naturally, the Five Books of Moses portrays the miracle as two separate words: *remember* in Exodus and *guard* in Deuteronomy. Only God can *act* in two contradictory ways simultaneously; we humans have been granted half the gift. We are privileged to at least be able to *think* of two conflicting things simultaneously. Fully under-standing this will greatly assist our ability to deal with conflict.

God's instruction to the ancient Israelites was that they should simultaneously guard and remember the Sabbath day. They were to *guard* it by scrupulously avoiding those activities that would diminish the day, such as using it for per-forming the same work as is done during the rest of the week. At the same time, they were to *remember* it by meticulously engaging in those activities that honor the day, such as eating celebratory family meals. To this very day once each seven days, heirs to that tradition observe the Sabbath both in the things we actively do and in the things we refrain from doing. In other words, "remember" tells us part of the story while "guard" provides another portion.

We humans obviously can not speak two words simultaneously. But we are given the uniquely human talent of being able to reconcile two seemingly con-flicting ideas. By thinking of a disagreement as a *maCH-Lo-Ket,* a part of the whole story, rather than as an argument writ in stone, we are often able to live in har-mony together, rather than seeing those who disagree with us as foes.

CHAPTER THIRTEEN

The Faith Factor

AMeN
אמן

M y father used to indulge my boyish love of the circus by taking me to the Big Top every time it visited our town. It wasn't until I became a father myself that it dawned on me: The real reason Dad regularly took me to the circus was that he loved the sawdust ring in the giant tent even more than I did.

The favorite part of our expedition was always the aftershow visit to the animal housing area. There we would wander past the elephants and their trainers. The lions and tigers would growl menacingly as we walked by. Our favorite animal was the horse that knew arithmetic. Perhaps my own futile attempts to master arithmetic at school lay behind my fascination with this creature. Just imagine—a horse that apparently could do sums of the sort that taxed my own academic abilities!

Once there, the trainer could usually be prevailed upon to show off his horse's mathematical talents a few more times. With his arm nonchalantly draped over the beautiful beast's neck, he would pose a question that would set my head spinning. To me it appeared that the horse was taking a moment or two to figure out the answer. Then the horse would begin tapping his foot...four, five, six times. Yes, that was the correct answer to the problem—six. And so it went time after time. The trainer asked an arithmetic question, and this amazing horse tapped out the solution.

The trainer always gave his horse a lump of sugar after each correct answer. I recall musing about how different school life could be were candy awarded each time we students cited the correct answer to an arithmetic question. I remained vaguely perturbed by those lumps of sugar. I also recall wondering why the man was called the "trainer" and not the "teacher."

I eventually found out that the horse knew no more arithmetic than I did. He had been trained (not taught) to tap his foot each time his trainer (not teacher) touched his ear. Each time he obeyed and tapped the required number he was rewarded with a sugar cube. This gave him incentive to continue translating ear taps into foot taps. In reality, he was only trying to obtain another sugar cube. Horses, like other animals, must be rewarded immediately if they are to repeat the trick.

DEFERRED GRATIFICATION

People, on the other hand, can drive themselves to achieve even if their reward is deferred. The more sophisticated we become, the longer the gap between effort and reward we are able to endure. After baby-sitting for neighborhood families, my nine-year-old and twelve-year-old daughters are happiest if they come home clutching their spoils. After school each day, my sixteen-year-old daughter works at a senior residential facility. She receives her paycheck every two weeks. But I have noticed that she can become pretty impatient as the end of the pay period dawdles closer—especially if there is a fashion sale at the local mall. Some of us insist upon being paid by the hour while others are reasonably content to work on a large transaction for a year or more before the payoff.

While the time gap may vary, in whatever way we earn a living we generally have to deliver before we reap the rewards. The farmer who plants and irrigates his crop might work for months before his harvest is sold at market. Then again, it might not sell at all. The craftsman who carefully constructs a bookcase will be paid only once the customer can take delivery. That, of course, depends on whether the customer approves of the product. The shoe store proprietor must courteously respond to the fashion aspirations of the fastidious buyer, after which, if he is lucky, he may make a sale. We intuitively grasp that only failure awaits the person who demands guaranteed payment before delivering. We recognize that anyone wishing to participate in the economy has to be willing to work first and then hope for reward. Nothing is assured, and every enterprise contains risk. It is almost as if built into the very system that sustains us is the need for *faith*.

Through His language, God notified us of His program in advance. A participant in the economy, perhaps a craftsman or a businessman, is known as an *UMaN*, spelled *aleph, mem, nun*. The same three letters pronounced differently form a word we use frequently in worship—*AMeN*. A person who is faithful is known as a *ne-EMaN*, and by responding to a prayer with "amen" we include ourselves among those who have faith.

Through this connection of business and faith, Hebrew informs us that faith is the one essential tool necessary to function effectively in economic interaction with our fellow humans. It is what is known as the risk element. This is an inviolable rule: If a particular investment carries zero risk, it demands zero faith and will return zero profit. From the viewpoint of the customer, nobody will guarantee payment for something he has not yet seen.

Perhaps we ought now to try to define faith. First, let us distinguish between *Faith* and *faith*. Not every usage of the word *faith* is within a religious context. The word *faith* itself simply means the ability to see something presently still invisible as clearly as if it were already there.

You might display ordinary faith in a city bus schedule by being at the bus stop on time. The farmer has faith that if he plants and cares for his crop, it will grow and he will be able to harvest and sell it. Without that faith, he would never even venture out to his fields. The craftsman has faith in his ability to construct an appealing product. The shoe store proprietor has faith that if he courteously demonstrates his new line of footwear to as many customers as possible, he will eventually sell out his stock. And anyone who invests in a stock, a bond, a mutual fund, or in any other kind of investment does so because his research and due diligence give him faith that the investment will pay off.

Does faith mean that every farmer will always successfully sell his crop or that every investment will succeed? No, of course not. However it does mean that without faith, no farmer would plant anything and no investor would ever risk his carefully accumulated capital.

The good Lord appears to have arranged matters so that faith, the ability to clearly see what is still invisible, is rewarded. Why would He do this? Possibly in order to reward Faith in Him. Religious Faith refers to the ability of the faithful to see God clearly.

EXERCISE STRENGTHENS THE FAITH MUSCLE

You see, all of our muscles are strengthened by exercise. What is more, any muscle strengthened by one particular exercise can be used for all kinds of other valuable exertions, most of which look nothing like the original exercise that developed the strength in the first place. For instance, I might work out with weights in the gym twice a week. One weekend my wife might ask me to help her rearrange the furniture. Watching this, my youngest child might ask, "Dad may be able to lift barbells, but who says he can lift chairs and tables?" The answer is that if I can lift weights of one shape, I am likely able to lift weights of any shape.

Similarly, our faith muscle is best exercised by regular expressions of Faith in God. I am not saying that no other means of strengthening the faith muscle exist; I am just saying that a relationship with God is probably the easiest and most effective way to strengthen our ability to see that which is not yet visible. Once our faith muscle has been strengthened in this fashion, it is much easier for us to use it in other areas, such as participating in the economy. One would therefore expect that any society in which Faith in God plays a major role would be a society that is conspicuously successful economically.

Could this perhaps be the reason why no atheistic regime has ever succeeded in generating an indigenous capital market? Having no Faith in God usually results eventually in no faith toward His creatures or their efforts. Could the AMeN principle also have something to do with the disproportionate success that Jews have always enjoyed in business? This principle may also explain how the United States has emerged as the greatest wealth-creating country in world history. It is, of course, also the country with the highest proportion of Faithful in the entire industrialized world.

Needless to say, both Judaism and Christianity place more emphasis on Faith than many other religions and thus benefit distinctively from the strengthening of the national faith muscle. The Bangladeshi peasant may possess some gold, but it is hidden in his mattress. It takes great faith, a practiced faith muscle, to hand that gold and all the time and effort it represents to a bank or an investment vehicle. With this scene multiplied by millions of peasants, we can see how a country can be impacted by faith or the lack of it. Without faith, that gold remains in the mattress and Bangladesh remains mired in poverty.

It used to be said that poor countries exist because of exploitation by colonial powers. It gradually became clear that colonies ended up costing money rather than producing it. England, for instance, never embarked upon her colonial adventures in order to swell the national coffers. On the contrary, literature of the period shows that England colonized other parts of the world in order to spread Christianity. Her involvement in Africa, Asia, and even America ended up costing the mother country great sums. So if imperialism did not cause some countries to be poor, what did?

The next theory was that creating wealth required both capital and information. In other words, to become rich, countries needed money to build factories and the know-how to build them. During the late twentieth century, international boundaries began falling until money pursued investment opportunity to every corner of the world. The Internet's spreading popularity meant that information also knew no boundaries. Well, with money available everywhere from Australia to Zimbabwe, and with information freely available to anyone with a computer, the question remains—why are some countries still poor?

The answer is surely AMeN. The creation of wealth requires some start-up money and the knowledge of what to do with that money. We do not need the Lord's language to tell us that. What we have not fully appreciated is that while those two prerequisites are certainly necessary, they are not sufficient by themselves. The creation of wealth depends on capital and information, PLUS a widespread system of faith. Everyone in economic interaction needs faith that their labor is likely to be rewarded. They need faith that the system under which they live will endure and that it will help them protect and preserve the rewards of their efforts. They also need faith that their fellow citizens will deal with them in what we appropriately call "good faith." Without that faith, all effort would cease, credit would never be extended, and the entire enterprise would gradually run down like an old-fashioned clock that nobody wound.

FAITH ON THE MONEY

I often enjoy posing a question to acquaintances in Europe and Asia that have never yet visited the United States: "There is a phrase we Americans post conspicuously, 'In God We Trust.' Where do we post this credo?" Not surprisingly, most people guess that we place this phrase on the walls of churches and synagogues. They are astonished to hear that it is to be found on our currency. I am not. The phrase is not needed upon the walls of churches and synagogues, for worshipers in attendance already know that. We need to be reminded on a daily basis that our very currency and the comfort it brings depends chiefly on Faith.

From the dawn of our national history we have always understood the connection between our Faith and our prosperity. This makes us a most unusual country and perhaps explains why our dollar symbol is made up of our national name—a letter *S* superimposed upon a letter *U*. The lower curve of the *U* coincides with the lower curve of the *S*, leaving us with a letter *S* beneath two vertical parallel lines, the original down strokes of the letter *U*.

AMeN, being both the noun *faith* as well as the verb *believe*—as in "I believe"—helps us understand this most crucial of lessons regarding economic comfort. A believer might utter "I believe" in the context of worship, while an investor might use exactly the same phrase to explain his choice of investment. It also teaches us the practical importance of first delivering and then getting paid. The Lord's language reveals His blueprint. He obviously wants us to first concentrate on doing something for other people and only thereafter to worry about what they can do for us.

What an incredible education to offer our children, and what a great lesson for us all to absorb. The world is set up to reward us to the extent that we focus on finding ways to do things for other people. If we focus only on what others can do for us, we fail.

Can you think of something material you would like? Who can't? Here is a much harder question: Can you think of something you could do for other people? Not so easy, is it? But when you thoughtfully answer that second question, you will have just written the first chapter of your business plan. Whether you plan a big public company or a small home business, the very first question to ask is, "What can I do that would really make other people happy?"

Isn't it obvious that God designed this system? How helpful of Him to give us the secret by making one word in His language mean both "faith" and "a participant in the economy."

CHAPTER FOURTEEN

Adding to Our Wealth

ASHIR-ESer

עשר

I f you start out with five apples and you give one of them to me, how many do you have left? Most likely you recall a similar arithmetic problem from your early school days.

The problem taught you the simple reality that the more you give away, the less remains for you. This is obviously true, yet we are struck by a mysterious paradox: How is it possible for the wealthiest nation in the world, America, to also be the only nation infatuated with giving money away?

This is not only true on an individual level, but it is also the case nationally. For instance Rotary, an international private organization of ordinary business professionals, raises an enormous amount of money through its American chapters. Through their donations of money and expertise, this amazing group has almost eradicated the dread disease of polio from India. Have you noticed that whenever calamity strikes anywhere in the world, American relief teams almost always arrive first? Invariably, America's charitable and faith-based organizations send generous assistance wherever needed.

Seldom do similar levels of assistance arrive from other countries. Many argue that since America is such a wealthy country, this is merely our responsibility. I think that the correct interpretation is precisely the reverse: We became wealthy because we were inculcated with a culture of charity in the cradle of our national infancy. Expressions of biblical morality, including a commitment to charity, are enshrined in the founding documents of the United States of America.

America is one of the only countries in the world in which charitable contributions are tax deductible. Some people incorrectly assume that Americans are charitable because of that tax rule. Again, the truth is precisely the reverse: That tax rule is in place to conform to the wishes of American citizens who wish to act charitably and do not wish to be doubly taxed. Large numbers of Americans donate sums that are greater than the levels that would benefit their tax status. The truth is that Americans are in love with the act of giving money away to those who are in need.

Try to count the number of nonprofit institutions in America that thrive only on the freewill offerings of their supporters. We have countless churches, schools, universities, hospitals, welfare organizations, and other nonprofits that cannot be found in other countries. We in the United States are imbued with the desire to give away at least a tenth of our money.

How did this come about?

America's founding fathers were quite familiar with the Lord's language. They knew that in Hebrew quite frequently only one word serves to convey what appear to be two very distinct English ideas. When that happens we are to realize that what seemed to us to be two separate ideas are not quite so unconnected.

In our case, the root of both the word *rich* and the word *ten* or *tenth* looks like this: *ESeR*. Thus we see that the idea of wealth is linguistically linked to "ten" or "a tenth." Both concepts are expressed by one and the same word.

THE PARADOX

Hence we gain one of the great breakthrough ideas of civilization—the idea of tithing, or giving away one tenth of one's money to others. By linking wealth to the concept of tithing, the Lord's language teaches us a wonderfully counterintuitive lesson. In some strange way, giving away a tenth of our money actually adds to our wealth.

The area of professional sales shines a light on this strange idea. Most sales professionals choose to be paid a commission instead of a straight salary. That way, the harder and more successfully they work, the more they will earn. Sales professionals are remarkable people. They trust their competence and their training and are willing to put themselves on the line. In essence, they say to a potential employer, "You should hire me because you have nothing to lose. You will pay me only after I have made money for you. I will only take a percentage of what I bring in." They are among the most important people who keep the wheels of our economy turning, and their magic is the commission system of payment.

The Lord's language encourages us to view our own means of earning a living as a sort of "commission" arrangement with God. But He offers an incredible payback plan—a 90 percent commission! Instead of keeping only 10 percent of every dollar I produce, as happens when I work for most bosses, my heavenly Boss allows me to keep 90 percent of every dollar. The remaining 10 percent, however, must be passed on to the Boss by giving it to His designated assignees: the poor and the needy. That is an authentically American way of viewing our charitable activities. We deserve no medals for giving away 10 percent of our money. It did not belong to us in the first place. We are just passing it through to its rightful owners.

The Hebrew language identifies this process of donating 10 percent, or tithing, by the same root word we use to indicate "wealthy." In other words, paradoxically, this process of taking away from what you have does not leave you with less, but causes you to amass more! Amazing! How can diminishing what we have, by giving it away, produce more for us? To understand this phenomenon, talk to any generous philanthropist, or even carefully examine your own charitable history. You will always discover the same startling story. People repeatedly prosper after starting to maintain a regular tithing program.

Television viewers may be familiar with a large and magnificent church in Southern California. Many years ago, prior to the church's construction, its pastor encountered the owner of a small business on a flight. They introduced themselves and chatted. As the flight progressed, the businessman became entranced with the pastor's vision of a great new church. He finally indicated to the pastor that he would like to assist in some way. The pastor suggested a large sum that was way out of the league of this rather modest businessman. As the businessman told me the story, he related how something inside him made him agree to pledge the extraordinary sum over the next year or two. Returning home, he told his wife of his very major commitment. Instead of feeling crushed by a burden that was entirely disproportionate to the family's budget, both he and his wife felt elated. They agreed that they would pay their pledge in the form of a strict tithe on all their business income. That way, he said, fulfilling the pledge became God's problem rather than his. He felt quite liberated by his tithing commitment—a commitment that continues to this day.

Today that businessman is a famous investor and a pioneer in several cutting-edge technical companies. He attributes his wealth and economic success entirely to his tithing commitment. Like so many other Americans, this man learned a true biblical lesson. Giving a tithe from your time and assets will lead to more, not less, wealth.

DEDUCTION MEANS GAIN

How can this illogical principle be true? This is the kind of mathematics that almost got me thrown out of grade school! But it does work and here's how. First, some background.

One of our basic problems as human beings is how to wrest a living from a sometimes reluctant world using the least possible effort. That simple question lies behind most economic activity. You might be watching a subsistence farmer on a small plot of land somewhere in Africa or three thousand early-shift workers streaming through the gate of a petroleum refinery in Texas. It doesn't matter. They are all doing the same thing: attempting to ensure food in their tummies and a roof over their heads in the most painless way available to them. You and I do pretty much the same thing.

Anyone supporting himself by subsistence farming doesn't have too many alternatives. It is not a desirable way of earning a living. You work seven days a week, 365 days a year. Your productivity is just keeping ahead of your most basic needs—if you are lucky. How would you escape subsistence farming? The only way is the Lapin "Three Cs" method: connect, communicate, and collaborate.

There is a well-known fourth C that grew out of the first three. It is the modern corporation, one of the keys to Western prosperity. That is exactly what a corporation is. It is a place in which many individuals can connect with one another, communicate with one another, and collaborate with one another. In so doing, they help one another earn a living in ways far more pleasant than solitary subsistence farming.

Interaction with others is the first and perhaps the most important step in creating a personal revenue stream. Without meaning to sound too metaphysical, we need to establish great big "money pipes" between us and the world out there. I am using pipes as a metaphor for the actual lines of communication that are so critical for our economic success. Of course, it is a mistake to establish links with only those people who might become direct instigators of our hoped-for revenue stream. We should try to expand our connectivity with everyone, not just potential employers or customers. One reason for this is because people talk to other people. The word spreads. We call this process networking.

START THE FLOW

Remember those pipes I spoke of? They represent our attempts to reach out into the world from which we hope to earn a living. Now you may have no way to persuade someone to build a pipe to you and start pumping money through it into your bank account. However, you do have the ability to build such a pipe yourself—and *you* can start pumping money through it.

"Wrong direction!" you might yell at me. No, I can assure you, the direction of the flow doesn't matter. You see, once you have built the pipe and started using it by sending money through it, the direction is immaterial. The key is to open up pipelines between you and the world around you. Once those pipelines exist, it is far easier for money to flow your way, too.

To translate the metaphor: Start tithing. Give at least 10 percent of your income to worthy causes. No sooner will you begin pumping money out than you will start to see money flowing in your direction, too.

Think about it. It is almost impossible to become charitable without meeting lots of people. In addition to the direct recipients of your largesse, there are those who staff the organization that arranges things. Don't forget all the other donors you will meet. Whom do you suppose they will choose to do business with? I am not for a moment suggesting that the only reason to perform acts of charity is to benefit your bank balance. Neither am I suggesting that those wonderful fellow citizens of ours who involve themselves in charitable organizations are doing so for ulterior motives. I am simply explaining the principle behind why the Lord's language uses the same word for charitable giving and wealth and explaining the mechanism by which that principle may apply.

One thing is for sure. Americans have been blessed by their adherence to the strange mathematical model that decrees that if you have ten apples and give one to someone who has none, tomorrow you will have fifteen apples. Have you been missing that blessing? Begin today to give generously and wholeheartedly, and then watch what happens.

CHAPTER FIFTEEN

Feel the Compulsion!

AVoDaH

עבדה

Once upon a time, a pair of nineteenth-century railroad laborers, Bill and Jeb, were laying track in the desolate wilderness of the American West. This is about the hardest work you can imagine, and the two were old-timers. They'd been laying track for decades. One day a surprise visit was made to the work site by no less a dignitary than the president of the railroad himself. While inspecting the work that was going on, the great and august man came upon our pair of dusty laborers. His eyes lit up.

"Well, hello Jeb!" he said. "You old scoundrel!"

Jeb looked bashful at first, but then the railroad president threw his arms around the exhausted laborer. He asked about Jeb's wife and family, shook his hand warmly, then finally moved along to complete the inspection.

Bill was amazed. "When did you ever know *him?*"

Jeb explained that thirty years earlier the two of them had worked together laying track. Needless to say, through the intervening years the other man had enjoyed greater career success than had poor old Jeb.

"So," asked Bill, "what company were the two of you working for back then?"

"Well," Jeb replied, "he was working for the railroad."

"What do you mean 'he was working for the railroad'? What about you? What were you working for?"

"Oh," said Jeb, looking a bit wistful, "I was working for fifty cents a day."

Some of us work just for the money. For others, work is a great opportunity.

The Lord's language has a word that means work: *AVoDaH*. This word also means "service"—in the dual context of the service in a restaurant and of a worship service.

The three letters that make up the root of the word are *ayin-bet-daled* (remember that the letter *ayin* can sound like an *a* or an *e* while *bet* can sound like a *b* or a *v*). Now the meaning of some Hebrew words, including AVoDaH, can best be grasped when we analyze the basic structure of the word. Instead of just accepting it as an ordinary three-letter root, we need to probe at a deeper level.

First of all, the first and last letters of this word comprise a sort of miniroot of two letters. They stand for an idea that is retained in many other similar words that start and end with the same two letters, regardless of which letter occupies the middle slot.

In our case, for example, the first and last letters of AVoDaH are the letters *ayin* and *daled*. Pronounced *EyD* (or "aid," as in "financial aid"), this little word at the root of our word for work/service means "witness." Some of the other words that are similar to work/service in that they start and end with the letters meaning witness are the words for future, *(ATiD)*, stand up, *(AMaD)*, and to bind, *(AKaD)*.

Confused? Don't be; another way to put what I've just explained is to say that witnessing *(EyD)* is an activity that somehow forms the common spiritual link between four related themes: doing service or work *(AVoDaH)*, being in the future *(ATiD)*, standing up *(AMaD)*, and binding *(AKaD)*.

WITNESS

What does a witness do? Before a judge, jury, and anyone else present, he gives testimony regarding an experience he has had or facts he knows. He may have witnessed the defendant committing a crime, or he may have witnessed him sitting on a park bench in New York at the precise moment the crime was committed in Los Angeles. He will present testimony about these things. A witness who gets up before the court and spouts irrelevancies or private opinions ("Your Honor, wow, did I see a terrific movie last night!" "Well your Honor, what I believe is...") will quickly be admonished to stick to the facts of the case. From a witness, anything that is merely personal is useless. What's needed from a witness is information that is more important than the witness himself. The reason a witness might be treated as a minor celebrity or placed in some elaborate witness protection program has nothing to do with how charming or witty he may be. He is important only on account of the testimony he will offer. His function, you could say, transcends his own individual importance.

In fact, to stress this importance, a court witness will typically take an oath binding him to "tell the truth, the whole truth, and nothing but the truth" before giving testimony. That binding oath makes him a *witness* rather than just a person with an opinion. We emphasize that being a witness "binds" you to testify. If you are reluctant, you can even be officially summoned to the courtroom. Once there, you are again bound to tell the truth. Do you recall that one of our four related words was "bind"?

We might say, then, that witnessing includes: an element of transcendence, that is, to say something that takes you out of and beyond yourself; and an element of binding, or compelling the witness. You will now see that all four words spun off from the two-letter root for witness, or EyD, are marked by precisely these two qualities.

THE FUTURE

Thinking of the future (ATiD) forces and compels us to transcend the present and recognize that in the blink of an eye the present will become the past. The present does nothing other than seize the future and instantly turn it into the past. Focusing on the future forces us to try to make the present a worthwhile moment. Thinking of the future forces and compels us to use it in order to prepare for future necessities. In fact, this three-letter root ATiD can also mean "to prepare thoroughly."

STAND UP

Standing up (AMaD) forces the body from its resting, supine state to an alert state of readiness. The symbolic meaning of a person's body when it stands also alludes to transcendence. When somebody stands up for something he believes, that something tends to be a belief about realities that transcend him for which he may even be willing to fight and die, such as beliefs in God or country. A person doesn't stand up for a mere taste or preference—say, for chocolate over vanilla. This is why we stand whenever we do things that are really important, things that have to do with our central beliefs and values. For instance, we stand while reciting the Pledge of Allegiance. We might stand for a moment of silence in memory of departed heroes.

BIND

The verb *to bind* (AKaD) will cause many of us to recall the story of the "binding" (AKeDaH) of Isaac, son of the patriarch Abraham. In the book of Genesis,

Abraham receives from God a command to bind Isaac on an altar and slaughter the young man as a sacrifice. The command was ultimately withdrawn, but not before Abraham had indeed bound his son with ropes for the most transcendent reason of all: because God wished him to do so.

Simply tying something up for no greater purpose than to keep it in one place would not be described in Hebrew by the word AKaD but by another root altogether: *kuf-shin-resh,* pronounced *KeSHeR.* This is the word we use in describing the task of fastening our shoelaces, for instance. When we are bound, physically or spiritually, compelled and forced by a purpose greater than ourselves, that is an AKeDaH.

Each of the words that grows out of the word for "witness" carries the implications of something higher than oneself and also of an unbreakable commitment. So it is with our word for service/work—AVoDaH. What lesson does this teach us that could be useful as we set off for work each morning? It teaches us the difference between working for the company and working for the money. It really teaches us the essential difference between work and drudgery. Why should we think of the former as wonderfully worthwhile but the latter as soul shattering?

TOIL VERSUS WORK

Herein lies the enormous difference between toil and work. A drudge works for his daily bread and that is all. He takes little pride in his effort and enjoys little sense of achievement upon its completion. This could apply to quite a few people in the modern-day workforce, right? What's more, drudgery has little to do with income. You can be a journalist, a dentist, a truck driver, or a schoolteacher and still be a daily laborer just the same.

In my corporate educational programs, I teach a principle that I call the cathedral concept. It is based on a famous story told of a traveler who encountered a workman fiercely pounding away at a stone with hammer and chisel. When asked what he was doing, the angry man put down his hammer and answered in a frustrated tone, "I am trying to shape this stone, and it is backbreaking work."

The traveler found a second man doing similar work. He appeared to be neither particularly angry nor happy. When asked what he was doing, he paused in his hammering and replied, "I'm shaping a stone for a building."

A third worker was singing happily as he chipped at his stone. "What are you doing?" he was asked.

Without missing a beat of his mallet, the worker responded, "I am building a cathedral."

The first person felt diminished by his work, like a slave. The third man found his work uplifting. They were doing the same task; it was their attitudes that differed. Many people are frustrated by jobs that they perceive as too small for their spirits. They may suffer and tolerate a job, but they yearn for a calling. Grinding away on a daily basis is intolerable, but work can be wonderful.

But how do we convert drudgery into work? Without question, part of the obligation for this conversion falls on the employer. However, as an employee there is still much one can do to convert one's job into a calling and one's labor into work.

The first and most important thing is to take the lesson of AVoDaH to heart. AVoDaH, work, must have two vital elements. First, it must lift one out of oneself; we call this a "transcendent" component. And second, it must also carry a sense of compulsion. In my cathedral concept story, the third worker associated both of these features with his task. He was not just working—he was building something. And he was not building just anything—he was building a cathedral! It was something much more important than his own being. He felt good, as we all might, at being an important part of a project of such magnitude and importance. He also felt driven and compelled to continue regardless of how tired he might have been. He didn't even take advantage of the passing traveler's inquiry to pause in his work.

Certainly, our employers can and should do much to improve our morale and our enthusiasm for our work. But let us assume they won't. It is up to us. What shall we do?

First, identify the ultimate purpose of what you do, and find out how it brings benefit to others in society. Don't get bogged down in the mechanics. If you are a journalist, you are doing much more than merely stringing words together. If you are an assembly-line worker, you are doing much more than merely fastening bolts. If you are a truck driver, you are doing far more than merely racking up the miles.

Next, try to start thinking of yourself as absolutely vital to the larger goal of your enterprise. Welcome the pressure this puts you under. Try to do just a little more than the job calls for. Try to achieve a quality of work far above "good enough." Feel the compulsion!

One might even say that there is redemption in the work of someone who regards himself as working for more than his daily bread. Redemption may come in the form of material success. When you work just for the money, money itself tends to elude you. When you work for an idea that you love—usually an idea about the future, not just your own future but the future of other people as well—wealth tends to appear in your hands almost unbidden.

WORKING FOR THE BOSS

But there is spiritual redemption, too. Work can grant us a greater appreciation of what it means to have a Boss. Not just the human boss over in the corner office, but a really important, heavenly Boss. This Boss has extremely high expectations of His employees and watches them constantly. Consider the advice you might give a high-spirited adolescent seeking a summer job. He is going on interviews; he even gets hired occasionally but fails to retain the job for very long. He asks you how to get a job and keep it. You might give him three critical pieces of advice:

- Show up for work reliably and punctually.
- Humbly do exactly what you are told.
- Behave respectfully to your boss, fellow workers, and customers.

None of these rules are terribly complicated, are they? Yet the majority of entry-level workers who get fired lose their positions for violating these rules. We are not talking about advanced vocational training here. We're talking about rules that have more to do with character training. In addition, the qualities we develop within ourselves as we convert drudgery into work are spiritually redemptive qualities. Imagine someone who has never before worked for a human boss. Not only is he ill-equipped to be his own boss, he is even ill-equipped to have a real relationship with his heavenly Boss. It all ties together.

If you can always view yourself as working not only for your mortal employer but also for your Boss in heaven, the weight lifted from your tired shoulders will be too great to be calculated. You will never find yourself working for a mere wage, but with a bigger picture in mind.

You will also be protected from the opposite extreme—that of labeling your work as an all-important career that takes priority over everything else in your life. If you have the proper attitude toward earning a living, everything you do will fill you with the thrill of purpose.

PART FOUR

GROWTH

AND SUCCESS

CHAPTER SIXTEEN

The Road to Happiness

SiM-CHa

שמחה

A s a beginner rabbi, I naively assumed that only destitute people sought refuge in drugs and alcohol. It was not until my friend Michael Medved and I established our synagogue in West Los Angeles that I discovered that there was no shortage of alcoholism and drug abuse among the affluent as well.

How can this be? I wondered. From what did those Californians living in the lap of luxury need to escape? I saw them at the University of California in Westwood. I saw them among the successful wheelers and dealers of the entertainment industry, and I saw them on Venice Beach near our synagogue. Why were so many, among the luckiest generation of Americans, walking around during the day in a drug-induced haze and falling asleep every night in intoxicated stupors?

The great psychiatrist Karl Jung pointed out that the old Latin name for alcohol, *spiritus*, hints at the answer to this problem. People depend on chemicals such as alcohol and drugs in order to assuage their suffering not from a material void, but from a spiritual one.

Apparently there is a form of poverty that is even worse than not having enough money in your pocket; it is the poverty of not having enough in your soul. The pain we experience when we lack that deep, internal happiness can be only temporarily anesthetized by means of chemicals. Unfortunately, the aftermath generally leaves us feeling even more empty and hollow. The next time we need a little more of the chemical, or perhaps a stronger chemical. Pretty soon the periods of time between dosages shrink, and the dosages themselves grow bigger. Eventually the problem becomes bigger than the pain.

THE NONCHEMICAL SOLUTION

There is a better way out of depression, sadness, and self-loathing, and it has to do with growth. A sense of achievement is the natural, organic, nonchemical solution to our spiritual void. Forget the tablets, the bottle, or the syringe. Find a way to fill the hollow space in your soul with a sense of progress, and all will be better.

How does all this work? First, we should examine the source of this knowledge, which is *SiM-CHa,* the Hebrew word for "happiness." The three root letters *shin, mem,* and *chet* mean "happiness."

We have a general principle in Hebrew that the two letters *tzadde* and *shin* enjoy a special relationship. The former stands for righteousness and represents a saintly individual, while the latter, shin, with its appearance of three tongues of flame leaping heavenward (ש), represents ultimate attainment of heavenly bliss through closeness with God. The special relationship I alluded to springs from the observation that we would expect the tzadde, the righteous person, to be seeking the shin, or heavenly condition. Thus, when we encounter any word that starts with either of those two letters we should also study its mate, the word that is otherwise identical but for its starting with the other letter. This pair of words will reveal its inner meaning when we recognize that the word starting with the tzadde precedes the word that starts with a shin. You could say that the tzadde word leads us to the shin word.

In our case shin, mem, chet means "happiness." The word that precedes it or leads us to it is tzadde, mem, chet, which means "growth." That's right. Growth leads to happiness! Our souls simply reject stagnation. Deep down, we rebel when the feeling that we are going nowhere subconsciously overwhelms us. When each day seems to follow upon the next with no progress that really matters, most of us humans find our spirits shutting down.

One obvious solution is to reintroduce an element of meaningful growth back into our daily schedule. That is easier said than done. In fact, it is a real challenge. Perhaps that is why so many go for the other far easier if sadder solution—suppressing that uncomfortable link between growth and happiness by means of chemicals.

Another piece of wisdom about happiness is revealed by the structure of the word. The three root letters can be arranged as the first letter, followed by the remaining two letters which comprise a short word, like this: shin and then mem, chet. The final two letters spell out the Hebrew word *MoaCH,* meaning "brain." Shin, as we have already learned, means striving heavenwards. Taken together then, the Hebrew word for happiness carries an additional meaning: Ultimate attainment of heavenly bliss is through your own brain. In other words, except for rare chemical imbalances, being happy is an act of mental will on your part.

What an astounding novelty—my happiness does not depend on anyone else! No other person in the entire world has power over my state of happiness. Happiness is not a state of mind brought about when *others* create an environment that I favor; it is just a decision I make, no more and no less. My happiness need never depend on anyone or anything. What an enormously liberating idea! For the vast majority of people happiness is a choice, and the road to achieving it is marked by growth.

NEITHER EASY NOR IMPOSSIBLE

It would be helpful to note that there are two general rules about the Torah: First, no commandment exists that requires us to do anything that comes naturally. For instance, there is no commandment or *mitzvah* in the Torah that requires God's people to breathe regularly for good health. Breathing comes naturally to us and requires no special commandment.

Second, no commandment is impossible for people to obey. Hard maybe but not impossible. Thus if you come across any commandment that seems quite easy, even natural, you can be sure that you do not fully understand the instruction. Honoring your parents seems too easy and natural? You probably are not even close to fulfilling what is required.

The second rule assures us that nothing God commands is impossible. For example, in the tenth commandment we are told not to feel a desire for things belonging to other people. My instinct is to respond by saying, "I can't help the way I feel! I will certainly obey the prohibition against stealing other people's possessions, but I cannot prevent myself from coveting them." Wrong! We are quite capable of controlling our thoughts and our feelings. It is not easy, but nobody ever said that the ultimate program for developing human potential would be easy. It is not *easy,* but it is *possible.*

Similarly, the Bible commands us to be happy. My instinctive response is: "I feel miserable. I cannot help how I feel. Perhaps if you give me the things I want, then I'll be happy." Wrong again! We do have the capacity to obey all commandments without any outside assistance.

If it is possible for humans to obey the commandment to be happy, how is this accomplished? We saw the clue a bit earlier. Unless we want to head down the dangerous path of chemically induced happiness, we will have to depend on personal growth to produce the happiness we pursue. How do we deploy the growth-equals-happiness principle?

One way to do this is to set yourself a daunting challenge. The more difficult it is, the more of a sense of accomplishment you will experience and the more happiness will result. It could be a physical challenge such as maintaining an exercise regimen or a rigorous diet. It could also be a moral challenge.

Perhaps you realize you have acquired the unfortunate habit of gossiping about other people. Try setting yourself the task of not talking about a single human being for an entire week. Perhaps you tend to procrastinate. Well then, challenge yourself to attend promptly to your work. Whatever it may be, seek a tough challenge. By embarking on this program and building success upon success, you will find an almost inexhaustible reservoir of happiness to draw from.

Our state of happiness truly is dependent upon feeling a sense of steady growth and progress in our lives. One reason some women feel a sense of depression after giving birth is that, up until that moment, they are constantly participating in the ultimate miracle of growth. While still pregnant, the mother-to-be is almost effortlessly engaged in progress and growth. That is why so many women enjoy being pregnant; it is hard to think of a more profound contribution that anyone could make. As soon as her baby is born, however, it all changes. Now in order to maintain the same ongoing growth, Mom endures sleepless nights and incessant demands. It is no wonder that some mothers experience depression at this unexpected turn of events.

HAPPINESS OR FUN?

In our pursuit of happiness, which is certainly a morally legitimate endeavor, we must always be vigilant to distinguish between happiness and fun. Here is a quick and easy way to tell the difference: Fun is usually pleasurable at the time but leaves a slight feeling of emptiness and waste following the activity. (Think of an entire afternoon spent watching television, for instance.) Happiness is usually a little more demanding while you're engaged in the activity or thought, but it leaves you with a wonderful sense of contentment.

Interestingly, the Lord's language has no word to describe fun. If you are not surprised to hear that, it means that you are becoming quite accomplished at spotting the lessons in Hebrew! Let me explain the appeal of fun and how easily it can be mistaken for happiness. Think of motion as a metaphor for growth. Our bodies can only sense movement if the velocity of our motion changes. With our eyes shut, we are quite incapable of distinguishing between being stationary and moving smoothly and steadily. Have you ever sat in a railway carriage and been unable to detect whether your own carriage is moving or the adjacent train has started moving? That's because we cannot feel the difference between no movement and steady movement.

However, we can easily sense any change in our velocity. If our vehicle is picking up speed, even if we are blindfolded we feel ourselves being thrust backward. If the conveyance is rapidly brought to a halt, we feel ourselves flung forward in the direction of motion. Even if we are riding in a car that is sharply turning, we feel the change in velocity caused by our change of direction. The general rule is that we are acutely sensitive to any change in the conditions of our motion.

In similar ways, our spiritual beings are exquisitely attuned to any change in growth. If our condition is stationary and stagnant, we feel nothing. If, however, we experience rapid change in our spiritual condition, we feel it very strongly and the sensation is basically pleasant. The problem confronting us is that negative change can masquerade as fun and in the short term can feel even more pleasurable than the early stages of positive change.

REMODELING

Positive growth can also be compared to a remodeling project. The initial result is horrendous. You find yourself surrounded by excruciating noise, suffocating dust, and bedlam. Only when it is well under way do the benefits start to unfold. Similarly, the initial response to a physical or spiritual exercise program is frequently an intense desire to stop. But after persevering for a while, the positive emotions and benefits kick in. Growth and achievement that result from struggle, diligence, and sacrifice feel very good to us and make us feel happy down the road.

Unfortunately, the sensation we feel when surrendering to indulgence is immediately enjoyable. Gambling can be fun, but it seldom produces happiness. The appeal it exerts comes from the illusion of growth that it offers. You see, while it is easy for us to feel a change in our spiritual condition, it is sometimes difficult to sense right away whether that change is positive or negative. It is only later that we can tell. Just as in a car, we can sense that the car is changing velocity but the only way we can detect whether it is slowing down or speeding up is by checking to see in which direction we are being flung. With our eyes shut and our sense of direction disoriented, we might know the car is changing velocity but we'd never know whether it is speeding or slowing. Not until later, when the blindfold is removed, would we know what had taken place.

Some activities produce a superficial sense of fun while others produce a sense of deep, inner happiness. The best way to tell the difference ahead of time is to ask ourselves whether the activity will contribute to our growth and development in a worthwhile kind of way. The answer will point unerringly toward genuine and durable happiness. Even very poor people can be happy as long as it is only their pockets that are empty and not their souls.

CHAPTER SEVENTEEN

The Dangers of the Snooze Button

ChaLoM

חלם

Though I host my own regular radio talk show, *The Rabbi Lapin Show*, on 1300 AM in Seattle, I enjoy listening to other radio talk shows as well. One genre in particular entertains me. Generally airing in the middle of the night, these shows have listeners and hosts that seem obsessed with conspiracies and often identify numerous and varied "threats to civilization." I have heard of green Martians and mysterious black helicopters, but I have yet to hear the one truly frightening peril.

I believe that one of the greatest unrecognized threats to civilization is the feature found on most modern alarm clocks. I am referring to the snooze button. This devastatingly dangerous device may even have been anticipated by the ancient rabbis of the Talmud a millennium and a half ago.

No, I am *not* pulling your leg. The Hebrew word that casts a laser beam of clarity on this matter is *ChaLoM*, the word for "dream." The Talmud reports a very curious fact related to dreams. It observes that if upon rising in the morning a person cannot remember his dreams, he should be considered wicked. The Talmudic sages aren't pulling your leg, either. They are merely putting their collective finger on a problem that is ancient but that finds its ultimate modern-day technological crutch in the form of the snooze button on the alarm clock next to your bed.

Consider what the snooze button allows us to do. Before bedtime, we carefully decide what time to get up in the morning. Then, when technology does its job and the alarm goes off, our first action of the day is to procrastinate. We can even do so numerous times! By the time we actually clamber out of bed, it may be a full hour after we first hit the dreaded snooze button.

THE BENEFITS OF LEAPING OUT OF BED

Why do I refer to the snooze button as "dreaded"? What difference does it make if we leap out of bed or linger beneath the covers? There is a big difference between setting the alarm for six and snoozing in repeated cycles until seven and setting the alarm for seven and leaping out of bed on the first ring. One result of not getting up with alacrity is that we can't remember our dreams.

Try it yourself.

The time during which we doze following that first moment of wakefulness is when our dreams fade into mist and disappear from our memory. In order to remember our dreams, we need to keep our finger off the snooze button. And to understand why remembering dreams is essential, we need to look more closely at the Hebrew word for dream, ChaLoM.

Recall the Hebrew language principle that spelling Hebrew words backwards often yields opposing ideas. In this case we see that ChaLoM spelled backwards becomes *MeLaCh,* or "salt." This leads us on a fascinating journey of understanding.

Have you ever wondered why we find a saltshaker on most tables, but not a potassium or magnesium shaker? After all, our bodies need many minerals to survive, not just salt. Fairness alone would demand equal time for, say, calcium. You might respond by telling me that potassium, magnesium, and calcium are amply provided in any normal, balanced diet. And you'd be right. The problem is that more-than-sufficient salt is also provided in any normal, balanced diet, yet we still place saltshakers on our tables.

Salt is the only mineral we ingest in its pure state. In our normal daily diets we consume iodine, iron, and various nitrates. In fact, our bodies can't function if they don't get enough of these and many others. But all the minerals we require occur naturally in the foods we eat or are added during processing as in iron-fortified cereals. Salt is the only mineral elevated to a place of honor at our tables—even appearing in specially designed holders.

Amazingly, because the Hebrew words for salt and dream are the reciprocals of one another, understanding salt gives us greater insight into the concept of dreams. We need to ask how a dream might be the opposite of salt. Now I realize that such a question sounds like something you might hear in a particularly surreal dream, but bear with me.

In the complex scheme of biblical nomenclature, salt is a symbol. The Torah pictures the world for us as a realm of existence composed of four basic elements: mineral, plant, animal, and *medaber,* or "speaker," meaning human. This is similar to the children's game of Animal, Vegetable, Mineral, though the Torah resolutely distinguishes between animals and people, thus the fourth category. When the Bible wishes to allude to the mineral kingdom, it chooses the mineral that is more familiar to us than any other—salt.

This explains why salt played a key role on another kind of table: the altar on which animal sacrifices were offered daily in the Temple in Jerusalem. The book of Leviticus enjoined that most sacrifices were to be offered on the altar accompanied by salt. Though this may sound arcane, it is not at all. Entire books could be written about features of ancient Jewish customs that have found their way into the customs of the Western world, and the salt of sacrifices is a fine example. Each time you pick up the saltshaker on your dining-room table, your meal becomes a symbolic representation of the Jerusalem Temple altar.

But this leaves unanswered the question: Why salt? Why was salt integral to sacrifices? Why must it have an echo on our kitchen table? And what does any of this have to do with dreams?

MAP OF HUMAN EXPERIENCE

The answer to these mysteries lies in the four-part organizational pattern of mineral, plant, animal, and human. Thousands of years ago when the priests slaughtered cows and bulls and salted the flesh before offering it to God, they were evoking this pattern. The Temple altar became a miniature map of the whole of the human experience. Every primary ingredient of the world, each of the four main categories, was represented there. Animal, vegetable, human, and mineral: the animal being sacrificed; the grain accompanying the sacrifice being offered was the plant; human, in the form of the priests; and finally the mineral, salt. In our day when we place salt on our "altar," or dining table, we are replicating that ancient pattern.

The Temple ritual might on the surface have resembled nothing more than a comical looking barbecue, but it was elevated to dizzying heights of holiness. What converted these sacrifices from primitive procedures into national activities that preserved the morality of a people was that it was all taking place only for the sake of pleasing God. Of course, it was not God who needed the sacrifices but humans who craved the experience. By bringing representatives of every one of the four aspects of His worldly creation before Him, we acknowledged that everything on earth was a gift from Him, and we undertook to use that gift properly. Similarly today, our table can become a kind of altar when we dedicate what goes on at that table to higher, spiritual ends.

There is a world of difference between table conversation revolving around gossip and discussion that elevates and enobles us. There is no comparison between grabbing a bite on the run versus sitting down at a table carefully laid with dishes and cutlery. If only we knew to keep this in mind, our tables would become the most spiritually important places in our homes. After all, in order to stay alive, animals also feed themselves. We, however, can choose to eat as if we were animals, regarding meal time as nothing more than an occasion for physical survival, or we can take the opportunity when consuming meat, vegetables, and minerals to do something much more spiritual and profound. We have the opportunity to transform feeding into a uniquely human and godly action. This is accomplished by how we dine and what we talk about during the meal.

Understanding this brings us full circle back to the meaning of ChaLoM, dream. Just as the dedication of every aspect of our lives to a higher purpose is the most fundamental meaning of the Hebrew word MeLaCh, so too is this the ultimate meaning of ChaLoM, dream.

As I mentioned earlier, we should expect to find in the ChaLoM and MeLaCh some quality of oppositeness. The two ideas do indeed allude to infinitely separate aspects of our experience. On one hand there is salt, a mineral, the most base and physical of the four components of our world. We even refer to a person who is well grounded and decent as the "salt of the earth."

At the opposite end of the spectrum we have a dream, a familiar experience that is almost totally ethereal, disconnected from the realm of physical existence. Classifying someone as a dreamer suggests a lack of connection with the real world. The challenge that is captured by the linguistic connection between these two words is to try to dedicate both our ChaLoM and our MeLaCh to a reality that transcends both. We can keep our unique and God-given humanity in mind whether we are engaged in the most basic activities represented by salt or groping toward the intangible and the ethereal represented by dreams.

This may sound daunting, but ChaLoM and MeLaCh tell us that built right into us is a human need to dedicate everything we do to a higher purpose. Our food consumption can supply us with nothing but the nutrition necessary for our physical well-being, or it can be a spiritual activity bonding friends and family to each other and to God. We can see each new morning as another sixteen hours to "get through" until we can escape into sleep again, or we can leap up joyfully, with gusto, and begin living a passionate existence from the very second our eyes open. And one important way to monitor how energetically and quickly we are rising is to see if we can remember a dream we had during the preceding night.

RISE LIKE A LION

The very first sentence of the classic code of Jewish law, the *Shulchan Aruch*, advises us to rise early in the morning "like a lion, in the service of God." Being a servant of God is not like being an employee of a human boss or manager. Our bosses expect us to arrive at the office at a certain time, and after eight or nine hours we are expected to stop working and go home. Not so with God. By energetically and promptly rising out of bed, we are acknowledging that our actions throughout the day are dedicated to Him. In this way, whether we can remember our dreams serves as a key to understanding what sort of attitude we take toward life. As a thermometer can gauge our physical well-being, our morning rising habits can serve as a gauge of our spiritual well-being.

Let me illustrate with an old story.

A very prosperous, corpulent gentleman once visited a rabbi to discuss something that troubled him very much. How to put it? Well, the man just didn't feel up to snuff. He had considered the possibility of consulting a physician, but he was pretty sure the problem wasn't physical.

His main symptom was a generalized sense of ennui. He felt vaguely dissatisfied with life—though life had brought every material blessing a man could ask for. The rabbi listened closely, stroked his beard, and said "Aha. I see. Yes, I do understand what you mean."

"Rabbi," said the man plaintively, "what can I do to make myself feel better?"

Truth is, the man wanted from the rabbi the spiritual equivalent of a pill or a lotion—a quick fix that would solve his problem with a minimum of effort. The wise rabbi knew this and proposed a remedy.

"I want you to drink a glassful of dew each morning." He explained that this must be fresh morning dew, gathered at dawn each day, drop by drop, from the blades of grass on the expansive lawn outside the man's mansion. "Remember to gather it at the break of dawn, not later; otherwise the dew you need will have evaporated at the first rays of the sun."

The man went away satisfied. This was exactly the kind of thing he had in mind.

However, despite the glass of dew he drank religiously each day, the man felt no better than before. He went to see the rabbi and complained about the ineffective cure.

The rabbi listened, then asked one question: "How is the dew collected?"

"Well," the man replied, slightly puzzled, "it's very simple. Each night I direct eight of my household servants to rise before dawn and flick drops of dew off the grass blades outside my house into test tubes. When each has gathered as much as he can, the drops of dew are poured into a drinking glass. When I get out of bed later that morning, I drink the glass of dew, just as you prescribed. But, Rabbi, it's done nothing for me!"

"Aha," said the rabbi. "I see. Now I understand why this remedy has been ineffective. I should have specified that every last drop of dew must be gathered not by your servants but by you!"

Gathering dewdrops or remembering dreams—there are many possible proofs that a person has risen from bed each morning with no dawdling.

When the early transmitters of the Torah say that the person who doesn't remember his dreams is a naughty person indeed, they allude to the fact that he is limiting his day by surrendering to his physical desires. Indulging oneself physically can certainly feel good momentarily, as when one gulps a hamburger from a fast food restaurant instead of awaiting mealtime. The problem is that it produces a corresponding lowering of spiritual vitality.

There is a fundamental lesson here. We can add purpose and gusto to our lives by jumping out of bed the moment our eyes open. It is one of the healthiest, life-affirming things we can do. Rather than being groggy and irritable the rest of the day for the lack of that extra ten minutes in the sack, we feel great. Ignoring the snooze button and dining rather than merely eating—both help us avoid the purposelessness and emptiness that truly are among the greatest threats to civilization.

CHAPTER EIGHTEEN

The Road to Kingship

MeLeCH

מלד(כ)

F ew experiences in life are as illuminating as a high school reunion. If you have never attended such an event, I strongly urge you to do so at your next opportunity. What's more, should that reunion happen to be scheduled for the same night as the reunion of your college class, skip the college reunion and go to the high school gathering instead.

What you will see is fascinating. No matter what school you attended, there was a certain social hierarchy among teenagers. Somehow kids naturally divide into little groups—cliques, castes—which they instinctively know to rank in order from most to least cool. At the top are the jocks and other "beautiful" people—the most athletic boys, the cutest girls. At the bottom of the ladder are "nerds." When I was a boy these individuals flocked to the Chess Club. Now it would be the Computer Club, but the idea and the identity are the same.

Nothing much can be learned from a college reunion because, although you'll find your classmates a little richer, grayer, and fatter, they'll be basically the same people you knew from university days. There are few major reversals to be observed in identity or social station. By contrast, what you'll find at your high school reunion is that the social hierarchy hasn't merely been toppled; it has been stood on its head. Before, the football tossers and basketball throwers were on top;

now it's the bookworms. Today those former nerds are Internet millionaires; the jocks are seeking jobs at the companies owned by the nerds.

CAMPUS MONARCHS

For a few golden years of adolescence, those jocks were the monarchs of the campus, but their reign was doomed to end early because they never understood what it means to be a king. The kings are dead, one might say. Long live the kings.

In the Lord's language, a king is a *MeLeCH*. We would do well to understand the hidden meaning of that word. The spelling is significant, of course: *mem-lamed-cof*. The ancient rabbis of the Talmud taught that the word MeLeCH is really an acronym, with each letter standing for another word. Here are the words that make up the acronym:

- *moach (mem)*, which means "brain";
- *lev (lamed)*, or "heart";
- *caved (cof)*. I've often seen caved translated as "liver," but this is a poor rendition. While caved certainly is related to the body and bodily functions, this word is used to designate the whole range of physical appetites and desires rather than a specific organ. That is, it stands in contrast to one's intellect, or moach, and to one's emotions, which is to say one's heart—or in Hebrew, lev.

And this is the point of MeLeCH—because the order of the letters that form the acronym allude to the relative priority a king must assign to moach, lev, and caved. This is vital information not just for the one or two kings, but for you and me. We may not aspire to royalty, but—whether at home, in the community, or at work—we owe it to those around us to aspire to leadership. And that is what this life lesson is all about.

GOVERNMENT OF SELF

Any king who wants his rule to be long and successful must govern first himself and then his realm—primarily by his intellect and then by his heart, keeping his own appetites low on the priority list. And so it must be for all of us if we want to be successful in life.

Pathetic as they may have seemed at the time, the nerds you knew in high school had their priorities straight. They were all brain. You might even have noticed something vaguely ascetic about them. They didn't pay a whole lot of attention to sensual pleasure. They wore ratty clothes, neglected to take care of their skin, never quite got down the art of shaving or hair care. Now asceticism can be taken to unhealthy extremes, but a little bit of it, especially in one's schooling years, can have highly beneficial results down the road. Ask Bill Gates. At the very least, asceticism balances an unhealthy preoccupation with one's looks.

Those jocks, on the other hand, really enjoyed their high school years, didn't they? They obeyed the mood of America's youth culture and set out to taste as many of the appetitive pleasures of life as they could, from beer to sex. (Of course, I know there are plenty of teetotaling and sexually abstinent young athletes out there. I am merely employing the word *jock* as a theoretical model.) They paid ample attention to their lev and their caved, to the neglect of their moach. They obeyed the compelling call of their young bodies and fell victim to the siren of emotional seduction. But the reign of those monarchs ended on graduation day.

Just for fun, let's try an experiment. Let us apply here the rule that if you spell a Hebrew word from back to front, the reverse spelling produces another word whose meaning is the opposite of the word you started out with.

Intriguingly, when MeLeCH is spelled backward we get the letters *cof-lamed-mem*, which is pronounced *CaLeM* and means "shame" or "embarrassment." In this Hebrew word we can see its English derivatives: calumny and calamity. (Did you think I would suggest this experiment if I didn't know beforehand that the results would be instructive?) If we understand kingship as the ultimate expression of honor bestowed on a human being, then shame is certainly its opposite. If following our heads instead of our hearts brings us to aristocracy (in its good sense) and leadership, then following our hearts (or, perish the thought, our bodies) will inevitably lead to calamity and eventual calumny.

Remember, in Hebrew there are no coincidences. Therefore, since we found that MeLeCH is both a word in its own right and an acronym, we should naturally look for an acronym in the word CaLeM. You won't be shocked to learn that the words constituting the acronym are the same words we found in MeLeCH, but in reverse order. You may also have guessed that the lesson to be derived here is the converse of the lesson we observed in MeLeCH.

What is the road to kingship—to success in the lifelong struggle to fulfill our highest and best hopes and dreams? It lies in subordinating heart to head and appetite to heart. The road to failure is the same as the road to success but taken in the opposite direction. It lies in subordinating head to heart and heart to appetite.

One further quality any leader must display is the ability to rule himself before he can hope to have his authority accepted by others. People with military experience know this instinctively. By running his life according to the dictates of his head rather than his heart or body, the leader demonstrates quite clearly that he is capable of ruling himself. Another way of describing this most necessary of leadership qualities is self-discipline.

This applies not only to would-be kings in the sense that George V was king of England. If any person in any context wants to be a leader, he must think of himself as a king. This doesn't mean he should go around issuing high-handed rulings by fiat. Nobody follows leaders like that. A leader must have consultants. This is why, among the laws of kingship found in the Torah, we find the law that a Jewish king must at all times carry with him a scroll of the Torah. While we may and should have many trusted advisers in life, we can find no better counselor than our Creator.

BEAMS OF LIGHT

This idea was carried over into the theories of kingship developed in Europe over the past two thousand years. In the European nations, kings were regarded as ruling by divine right. A king who ruled without such a sanction was an illegitimate ruler. A king who could legitimately claim divine sanction declared himself a spiritual heir of Moses himself.

While the Jewish people have had many kings, most famously David and Solomon, our first king really was Moses. He never ruled explicitly under that title, but the Bible understands him as filling a monarchical role. When he descended from Mount Sinai, where he had been consulting with God for forty days, the text informs us that he had *karne ohr*, "beams of light," shining from his face. (Michangelo, basing his work on an imprecise translation of *horn* for the word *beam*, put horns on the his statue of Moses. This is the origin of the myth that Jews have little spiky horns growing out of their foreheads. Most of us do not.)

These beams of light constituted the first crown God ever bestowed on a monarch, and the kings of Europe emulated the Mosaic model by designing for themselves crowns from which spikes of shiny precious metal emerged—karne ohr. The idea was to artificially emulate the royal pattern, set by Moses, that a real king has beams of light emanating from his head. This was a sign of royalty and nobility and is behind our understanding of halos of light around the heads of great figures.

We would be wrong to think that only a man with a crown on his head or the title Chief Executive Officer on his office door can be a king. When Jewish law sets out the rules of kingship, it offers a model of what it means to be a MeLeCH, or king—whether in the boardroom or even around the humblest of family dining-room tables.

Fathers and those men who wish to be fathers someday should pay special attention here. One ancient Jewish law still practiced in many homes today declares that no one should sit in a parent's chair. If mothers and fathers are to receive honor appropriate to their roles as leaders of the family, a good place to start is with their throne or chair. A father's dining-room or living-room chair is no mere resting place for anyone to use while consuming food or reading. It must be his throne exclusively.

EVERY HOME A CASTLE

On the old TV show *All in the Family*, Archie Bunker was made a figure of fun because he had a chair in the Bunker family's living room that was exclusively his. His modern son-in-law mocked him for insisting on this right. But the idea of a father's special chair is actually very important. The point is not to elevate Dad alone but to uplift the entire family. In a family where the father is king, his wife by definition is the queen, and the children are princes and princesses. The family table becomes the site of royal feasts.

Many stories have been told about Jewish families who endured periods of great economic and social persecution. Tyrants and their mobs could take away people's money or even their lives, but they could not take away an individual's self-worth. In the face of deprivation and humiliation, Jewish families clung to the family as a place where father was king, mother was queen, and everyone else part of the royal family. Especially on the Sabbath in ghettos across Eastern Europe, the family converted their humble hovels into royal palaces by practicing the principles of leadership and aristocracy. Whatever the outer trappings, nobility will shine through when reason and wisdom trump emotions and instincts. To this idea of kingship we can and should all aspire.

CHAPTER NINETEEN

Conquer Your Fears

SHaNaH

שנה

A friend recently told me he planned to ask a certain young woman to marry him. He had made up his mind to pop the question, and knew the exact locale—a lovely beach overlooking Lake Washington—where he would offer her a diamond engagement ring, but he was uncertain *when* to do so. After all, this would be one of the most important days of his life, and he wanted the time—the place on the calendar—to be as special as the physical location.

It was approaching the season of Passover (in the spring), and to his surprise, I recommended that he propose to his beloved just before Passover began, an hour or so before nightfall and the start of the first holiday meal, or seder.

Why that day? Well, time is a slightly weird phenomenon. A young child who quickly acquires a sense of size and weight will have difficulty estimating time. With a little experience, he knows whether a particular package is likely to be heavy or light. Time, however, is less intuitive. It seems to take forever for a long-awaited vacation trip to arrive. Once embarked on that trip, though, it seems to pass by in just a flash.

Try this experiment: Ask a child to hold your city's telephone directory at arm's length while you time him for forty-five seconds. Then allow your young subject to munch on a favorite candy for exactly the same period of time before you confiscate it. Now ask the child which time period was longer. For most children, the time spent holding the phone directory will seem like an eternity. And most will incorrectly estimate that you allowed the candy enjoyment for a far shorter period.

Another way in which we misperceive time is the way we visualize its passage. We tend to think of time as a very long, straight railroad track, coming from nowhere and going nowhere, and that life resembles a train upon which we and our loved ones progress down that track. Upon that track are railway stations, representing notable dates like birthdays and holidays.

A LIFE-TRAIN SPIRAL

The reality is that while our journey through time may be compared to a railway track, it is *not* a long, straight track. Think of your life-train as traveling along a track laid in an ascending spiral or helix. It takes a year to traverse one complete circle, at which time you return to the same station you were in one year before. However, this time, the train has entered the next higher floor of this multilevel station. The stations are not conventional long platforms but large, multistory structures.

When my own life-train arrives once again at the Jewish holiday of *Shavuot*, Pentecost, I have returned to the exact day upon which my ancestors stood at the foot of Mount Sinai and received the Torah from God. The reason I do not run into my ancestors is that they are on one of the lower levels of the station.

Ah, I know what you are thinking: Couldn't I just take the elevator down and meet up with the ancient Israelites? It is not so simple. As I said earlier, our understanding of time is not intuitive. Nonetheless, the spiral staircase view of time serves us well.

Celebrating our religious, national, and family holidays each year helps to keep us linked to our timelines. We commemorate the passing of our parents, and we observe the days upon which great wars ended. Easter and Passover, July Fourth, and Thanksgiving recur from year to year. Each year we return to July Fourth, and it's Independence Day all over again—a different July Fourth from last year but still, mysteriously, the very same day.

I suggested that my friend propose to his bride-to-be on Passover Eve because in doing so he would be giving her a gift. She would always know that the anniversary of her engagement was doubly memorable for its having occurred on a day that Jewish people around the world already recognize as very special. Each year at Passover she would receive an additional boost of warmth, delight, hope, and love from remembering the day her husband proposed to her.

Holidays are funny. Just the change of date on the calendar fills our hearts with joy and expectation, or—sometimes, for people who are lonely, without the blessing of good friends and loving family—with sadness and despair. The high suicide rate at Christmastime is well known. If we are fortunate enough to associate the passing stations of our life with progress and achievement, then those milestones on our journey become happy events. Growing children, lasting relationships, and successful enterprises are just some of the things that add joy to the train ride.

SOMETHING TO SHOW

This may be one of the foundations of the photographic industry. One reason we all love collecting photographs of our families is that they prove to us on some deep level that we have something to show for the journey taken. Tourists do the same thing. After spending considerable sums of money and several weeks indulging in a vacation, we return home hoping to cajole some innocent friends into watching our videos or slides. Why do we feel a need to subject our friends to this torture? Mostly for our benefit, not theirs. We seek affirmation that all the time and money we spent did not evaporate into nothingness.

This is one of the great hidden benefits in remaining married to one person. Over the years memories accumulate and affirm that the ride along the tracks was not wasted. One of the most loving and evocative questions of a durable marriage is "Do you remember the time that we…?" Our psychic health demands that we constantly try to return to that same railway station we visited several circuits ago on that annual railway track. It may be an upper floor, but it is still the same railway station, and it feels warm and familiar.

The Hebrew word for *year, SHaNaH,* sheds light on the circular nature of the passing years and teaches us some important lessons in the process.

Actually, the Hebrew consonants that spell SHaNaH—*shin, nun, hey*—can mean other things besides year. (Remember that in Hebrew, as it's written in a scroll of the Torah, there are only consonants, no vowels.) These letters can mean "tooth" *(shein),* "two" *(shenayim),* or the verbs "to repeat" *(shanah)* and "to learn" *(shanah).*

In no other language can anything valuable be learned from the fact that certain consonants in a certain order are shared by different words. In English the consonants *c* and *p* can be used to spell the words "cop," "cap," "coop," and "cup"—but this fact is meaningless, a mere coincidence. A policeman (cop) has nothing in common with a piece of cloth you wear on your head (cap) or a home for chickens (coop). But in Hebrew, there are no coincidences. In fact, the language does not even possess a word to describe the idea of a coincidence.

Why would the Hebrew word for "year" also mean "two" and "repeat"? A year is indeed linked, first of all, to the idea of repetition, as I hinted earlier. Time only appears to be a long, straight railroad track if you think that life is basically meaningless; we're born, second by second we get older, and finally we die. But the truth is that we experience time as a cycle. Come Christmas or Passover or any anniversary or birthday, and we intuitively feel that we have repeated an experience, returning to a place in time that we had visited on exactly this day last year and for many years in the past, and as we hope to do for years to come. Of course, this year's birthday is not exactly the same as last year's. After all, I am 365 days older; the hair may be a bit grayer; the body a tad less lithe. But in important ways it is still the same day. So holidays and anniversaries repeat themselves, yet they don't. This is why I describe the passage of time as a spiral.

Okay, that's a nice observation, you're probably thinking. *What good does it do me? Where is the life lesson?*

Are you afraid of public speaking? Of flying in an airplane? Of riding in elevators? The Hebrew word-concept, SHaNaH will now come to your rescue. To show you how, let me ask another, seemingly irrelevant, question: Did you ever wonder why the back molar tooth that often pushes its way rudely into your mouth, sometimes requiring painful surgery, is called a "wisdom tooth"?

As I've mentioned already, certain ideas migrated over the millennia from their origin in the Lord's language, Hebrew, to other languages like English. These ideas were often conveyed in subtle nuances of word and phrase. What's a painful molar got to do with wisdom? In Hebrew a *shein,* or tooth, shares a three-letter root with SHaNaH, "to learn"—that is, "to get wisdom"—which in turn shares a root with SHaNaH, meaning "to repeat." Here's how the ideas flow one to the next.

VICTORY THROUGH REPETITION

We learn through repetition. Remember that fear of public speaking? Ask any competent psychologist how you should go about defeating a phobia like that. Probably after some learned and compassionate throat clearing, he'll tell you there's only one effective way: You must repeat the experience that you're afraid of, over and over again. Get up and speak before a group of people—again and again. Afraid of elevators? Go to your neighborhood skyscraper, get in an elevator, and ride it up and down, up and down, till the building manager suspects you of vagrancy and orders you to leave. Airplanes? Same thing. Professional phobia therapists make a nice living by taking people who fear flying on group tours of the airport. Therapist and patients spend a day going from plane to plane. They get on board, sit for a moment, then get off. Next plane, same thing. Eventually, the repeated experience becomes more familiar, more "learned"—and less stressful.

What's going on here? Through repetition we learn to subject our churning emotions to the calming power of our intellect—that is, to make our brain rule over our heart. The more often you perform a certain feared action, the more you learn that you have nothing to fear.

Repetition is essential to all learning. Just consider that wonderfully useful childhood educational exercise, memorizing poetry. Unless you happen to be blessed with a photographic memory, the only way to do it is by repetition. Remember the "wisdom tooth"? We get wisdom by deriving a lesson from our teeth. If you want to really learn a subject—or an idea, or a language, or whatever—there are two ways to do it. You can repeat it over and over again. In addition, you can chew it (so to speak) over with a friend.

In Jewish Talmudic schools, called *yeshivas,* the ancient, classic pedagogical method is called *chavruta* learning. (Remember, the word *chaver* means "friend" or "colleague.") One student is paired with another, his colleague in learning, and together they pore over the text of the Talmud, discussing it as they go. Not only is this a lot more fun than nodding over a book by oneself hour after hour, but it also improves the learning process immeasurably. Thus we see how learning is linked to "twoness," for two people can learn together more easily than can one alone. Together, they repeat, repeat, repeat.

Recall that SHaNaH, year, is also related to shenayim, two. For our teeth to work properly we need *two* sets of them, an upper and a lower set. With these, we grind our food until it's soft and small enough to digest. But anyone unfortunate enough to be stuck with only one set of teeth is worse off than if he had none at all. With no teeth, only gums, we can still (if rather slowly) gum our food, mashing it around until it's more or less digestible. But with just upper teeth, or just lower teeth, we would starve.

Learning works the same way. Two learners together can digest a difficult subject, while one learner by himself has a much tougher time of it.

So from SHaNaH we derive some very interesting lessons indeed: how to overcome our fears and how to multiply our power to learn. Do the lessons work? Try them and see for yourself. In the meantime, it's intriguing to note that this Hebrew word, SHaNaH, possesses yet another indication that buried treasure is contained within.

Get out your calculator. As I've noted elsewhere, Hebrew is unique among languages. When you convert its letters into numbers and add them up, the sums are peculiarly significant. Don't try this with English! For instance, taking the English word *year* and attempting to add up the numerical values of the letters doesn't get you far. The letter *y* is letter 25 in the alphabet, *e* is 5, *a* is 1, and *r* is 17. Add them and you get 48, which tells us absolutely nothing about a year. But the ancient science of Hebrew letter arithmetic, or *gematria,* informs us that when you add up the letters *shin* (300), *nun* (50), and *hey* (5), you get 355: namely—aha!—the number of days in a year.

Wait a minute, Lapin, you say. That should be 365 days in a year!

Yes, you're right if we're talking about a solar year—a year measured by the time it takes the earth to complete exactly one orbit about the sun. But for more than three thousand years, the Hebrew calendar has been lunar based, not solar. Each month represents the number of days it takes for the moon to circle the earth: twenty-nine days plus part of the thirtieth day. Twelve such months add up to—you guessed it—a 355-day year.

This lunar year, like the solar year, circles back on itself bringing with it all the holidays and anniversaries we love. My friend with the engagement ring decided to take my advice and proposed marriage to his beloved on Passover Eve. Each year for a lifetime to come, amid all the arduous spring cleaning which tradition-ally goes along with the weeks just before Passover, his bride will recall a day on the shore of Lake Washington. She'll be transported back through the years to that very same day, and she will be able to reexperience the wonderful moment when she said, "I will marry you."

PART FIVE

IDEAS

CHAPTER TWENTY

Trash or Treasure?

ReFeS
רפש

To this day, I have a hard time throwing that worn-out shirt or those old socks into the trash. Maybe you feel the same way.

Notwithstanding the frayed elbow on the shirt or the hole that's been growing for weeks around my big toe, I just find it hard to toss those items out. I can well afford to buy another shirt and another pair of socks, but I find myself putting them back in the drawer rather than in the garbage. I guess I'm subconsciously remembering how, when I was a kid, my mother also hesitated to throw out old clothes—not because she was cheap or because my family was poor, but because my mother simply felt that clothing deserved special respect. Maybe your mother was the same way.

Instead of dumping clothes that had passed their prime or gotten small indelible stains on them or had merely fallen out of style, my mother preferred to give them to charities. Much as they do today, these organizations would then turn around, and at a nominal cost, sell or sometimes give these donated articles of clothing to poor people. A coat or suit too tattered for us was a highly prized garment among folks less fortunate.

My mother—and yours too, I bet—also had the sense that there is something holy about clothing. Food and clothing are two necessities in life. But whereas food gives only physical sustenance, fulfilling a physical need, clothing fulfills both a physical need and a spiritual longing. It keeps us warm and also provides dignity. Somewhere in the consciousness of every civilized human being is the awareness that clothing is godly.

The very fact that clothing is uniquely human should give us a clue about this. The French poodle prancing alongside its madam in a little tartan vest that matches the coat on the other end of the leash looks ridiculous. After all, the Bible tells us that the first clothing any human being ever wore was created for Adam and Eve by no less distinguished a tailor than God himself. Animals have no need for clothing while, obviously, they do need food. The fact that we humans clothe ourselves no matter what the weather is a tribute to our intuition that we are godly creatures, not animals. This accounts in part for our discomfort in treating clothes as common household garbage.

But Mom also understood something else that fewer and fewer of today's freshly minted university graduates understand. Maybe old clothing ought not be trashed but an awful lot of other stuff should be! A line you hear all the time from people educated enough to know better is "Everything is relative." But my mother insisted that good was indeed good and evil was indeed evil. She had very little confusion about these two concepts. She had no hesitation about throwing out real garbage and throwing out evil and smelly ideas. I'm reminded of her lesson when I look at today's garbage industry.

A SACRED SACRAMENT OF SECULARISM

Dealing with the waste material of our busy lives used to be a simple utilitarian problem. We expected cities to pick up our trash and safely dispose of it. That was all. There was never any cause for reasonable citizens to genuflect at the altar of garbage. Get rid of it, and we don't care about the details. But recently, recycling has become almost a sacred sacrament of secularism. Garbage recycling is not being done because it is the smartest way to deal with garbage; it is being done for philosophical reasons. I reach this conclusion because recycling certainly has not yet proven to be an economic way to deal with our urban waste.

Several major cities in America inflict draconian recycling rules upon citizens who then meticulously and diligently sort their potato peels and empty cans into different color-coded containers, each of which must be put out for collection on a different day.

Later, all these carefully collated containers are emptied into the same city dump. These cities justify the charade by saying that soon economically viable ways of treating recycled garbage will emerge and then we shall have the collection system already set up. Meanwhile, we are all victims of a curious doctrine: Waste your time recycling so that city employees can waste theirs by combining everything you just finished laboriously separating.

Children at school are given the idea that recycling is more than just an efficient and economic way to deal with waste. Instead, they are told that there is something almost noble about recycling. Once they were taught that visiting sick people in the hospital was the way to do good; nowadays they are taught that the highest form of doing good is recycling. We need to recognize that there is a moral lesson being taught here: What's trash and garbage for one person may well be for an excellent acquisition for someone else.

You may think I am being too fanciful, but children are definitely being taught that almost nothing is garbage. Is this a problem? Yes, it is, because the underlying philosophy also leads to the thought that no *idea* is nonsense and all values and beliefs are equal to one another. Along with the notion that there is no such thing as garbage that should be discarded, we might also be gaining the notion that no *idea* is worth discarding either. Perhaps we are losing our ability to simply and confidently declare, "That is utter and complete nonsense!"

The Hebrew word for *trash*—ReFeS—is instructive on this subject. You'll recall the principle in Hebrew that, unlike in other languages, a word spelled backward does not become a meaningless jumble of letters as it would in English. For instance, "trash" spelled backward is "hsart" and "refuse" spelled backward is "esufer." Neither word means anything whatsoever.

But try this experiment: Reverse the spelling of the Hebrew word for trash. ReFeS is spelled *resh-peh-shin*. (*Peh* can be pronounced either as a *p* sound or as an *f*. *Shin* can be pronounced either as an *s* or a *sh*.) Spelled backward, ReFeS becomes *shin-peh-resh*, a root that can be vocalized (pronounced) in several different ways. From this root we get, above all, the word *SHaPiR*, which means "excellent" or "fine." It is also the origin of the Jewish last name Shapiro. You will hear in it the English word *super* just as, in ReFeS, you hear the English word *refuse* (pronounced with a hard *s* sound, meaning "trash" or "garbage"). The word *rubbish* comes from the same Hebrew root, easily seen once you know that in many languages, the letter *b* tends to morph into the letter *p* and vice versa.

Funny, isn't it? In the Lord's language, trash spelled in reverse becomes a word that means the exact opposite. In other words, Hebrew insists just as firmly as did Mrs. Lapin that the opposite of valuable things or ideas is garbage and wrong ideas. Some things are absolute after all.

Since I'm an enthusiastic sailor, I'll illustrate this principle about absolutes with a maritime example. If you are ever on a boat and the skipper tells you to grab and pull a certain rope on the *port* side of the vessel, you'd better make sure you know port from starboard. Pull the wrong rope on a boat and you are going to be in big trouble. You, and everyone else onboard, might need life jackets.

The word *port* does not mean "left" or "right." It means the side of the boat that's on your left *if* you are facing the bow. *Bow* doesn't just mean "front." It means the end of the boat that usually is first to slice through the water. If you are facing the bow, the side on your right is called *starboard*. But if you turn around and face the stern, it is now the side on your left that is called starboard.

You see, on a boat, left and right won't work because they are relative terms. That is why when you look in a mirror, it switches your watch from your left wrist to your right. If you have never done this experiment it is worth trying. Face a mirror with your watch on your left wrist, and in the mirror it will be reflected on your right side. Notice that the same mirror that moves your watch with such ease, fails to switch your necklace from your neck to your ankles. That is because up and down are fairly reliable directions, whereas left and right are not. If someone, while talking to you on the phone, tells you that she is pointing toward her left, you know very little. In order to know the direction in which she is pointing, you would need to know which way she is facing. Now, had she informed you that she was pointing toward the north, you would clearly understand. That is because north and south are absolute directions, as are up and down.

On a boat, we depend on everyone knowing what is going on. Perhaps that is why I so love being aboard a boat. During our family's summer boating trips, all my children effortlessly switch their lefts and rights into ports and starboards. It is not an affectation; they understand that left and right are relative, and Lapins are not crazy about relativity other than in connection with Einsteinian physics. Up and down are usable on a boat since they always mean the same directions regardless of which way you may be facing. But left and right? Never! Only port and starboard have absolute meaning.

RICH OR POOR?

Is everything absolute? No, of course not. Funnily enough, one area that is very relative is exactly one that many people consider to be absolute. I refer to these words we use so casually: "poverty" and "wealth." We often speak of poor people, but who are they? Our government's Department of Labor designates about 30 percent of Americans as poor. This is a statistical designation and has little to do with the fact that a significantly large number of those designated as poor own their own air-conditioned homes, cars, and more than one color television set.

It is very difficult to define poor when it comes to humans. You see, if an elephant needs a hundred and twenty pounds of hay a day to remain healthy and all he gets is sixty pounds, you could probably label him a poor elephant. But with people it is much more difficult. Some people choose to work sixty hours a week in order to increase their earnings. For others it is more important to have ample time to go hiking or watch television. Should the latter, who have chosen to work only twenty-five hours each week, be labeled poor? Should some of the income of the rich group be confiscated and given to the poor group, or should we instead recognize that humans make choices? Some people choose to spend all they earn on consumer goods, vacations, and restaurant meals. Others choose to live more frugally and invest their savings. Should the second group be considered rich and be made to help support the first group? These are tough questions; their complexity demonstrates that poor and rich are relative terms that do not really apply to humans.

Each one of us could look over one shoulder and see people who have much more than we do. However, we could just as easily look over the other shoulder and see people who have much less than we. Whether we ourselves feel rich or poor depends over which shoulder we are peeking. Anyone who thinks that no very wealthy people ever go to bed at night worried about money simply does not understand human nature. Some things like wealth and poverty are very relative, which is why most people are more comfortable living and socializing among others of the same general socioeconomic level. If we spend a lot of time among people who have much less than we do, we feel almost sinfully rich. If we spend much time among those with substantially more than we possess, we feel relatively poor. Neither sensation is terribly comfortable.

This is why we have the power to determine whether we feel rich or poor. It is all relative and therefore within our power to determine.

The same can be said of experiences. Instead of designating a bad experience as such, we can switch our perspective and try to make the best of it. Just as ReFeS, rubbish, can be viewed from the opposite end and turned into a precious stone, a sapphire (SaFiRe), so can some of the bad hands life deals us be turned around. Some of business and science's greatest achievements have emerged from what at first seemed to be major failures or setbacks. The most painful moments in our lives, the most unpleasant encounters we have with other people or with organizations, can be launching pads for the future.

We must be careful, however, to understand that this is not true for ideas.

Every idea does not automatically have value. There really is a great deal of garbage around, and the best thing to do with garbage is dump it. In doing so, we will find that we have more room and energy for that which is truly valuable.

CHAPTER TWENTY-ONE

Mr. Silverberg's Word Puzzle

EMeT

אמת

I take particular delight in teaching Hebrew to accountants. These dogged number crunchers get an unfair rap in contemporary culture. They are thought to constitute the most supremely dull profession conceived on this green earth, but actually the green stuff they take so much care in counting and recounting provides them with an ideal training program for understanding the Hebrew language. Mind you, it's not the money that does this, but the counting.

When I was a synagogue rabbi, I once had the opportunity to teach a little bit of Hebrew to a wealthy Beverly Hills accountant. We shall call him Mr. Silverberg.

I offered him a challenge. He had never properly learned Hebrew as a child and considered himself basically illiterate in that tongue. I told him that after I had taught him just a few simple principles, he would be able to figure out the meanings of Hebrew words on his own. Without a dictionary, just by using the mathematical intuitiveness he had gained as an accountant, he could quickly become proficient.

He looked at me dubiously, in the manner of all accountants when their clients are feeding them a line.

"Sure, you can do it," I assured him. "Let's take an example."

"All right," he agreed. "Let's do that."

I explained that I would tell him about the Hebrew word that means "truth" along with a couple of basic rules of Hebrew linguistics, and then he would be able to successfully predict for me the Hebrew word for the opposite of truth, "falsehood." He agreed to the challenge.

See if you can match his wits.

POSITION IN THE ALPHABET

In Hebrew, the word that means "truth" is *EMeT*, spelled *aleph-mem-tof*. The spelling is important because it provides an insight into the nature of truth. The first thing to notice is the position of these three letters in the Hebrew alphabet.

That alphabets have an order—a proper sequence, as in English where *a* is followed by *b* which is followed by *c* and so on—is not surprising. This aids children when they first set out to memorize the alphabet. Without an order, we would be left with nothing more than a meaningless jumble of letters, very difficult to commit to memory. But why this order in particular? Wouldn't it make more sense to start the alphabet with the letters that we use most often? Then the first letter of the alphabet would be *e* or *s*, not *a*. Instead, the English alphabet at least begins with the same sequence, as does the Hebrew alphabet: first *a*, which is similar to the Hebrew *aleph*; then *b*, which echoes the Hebrew *bet*.

Just as English has a first letter of the alphabet, and a tenth and twentieth—and these number equivalents never vary—so it is with Hebrew. The difference is that in English and all other tongues, the order of the letters is merely an aid to memorization. The spelling of a word, the numbers that correspond to the letters in the word and their precise order within the word and within the language, is meaningless in languages other than Hebrew. But in the Lord's language, letters and numbers and the way they correspond to each other are rich with meaning, tapping into mystical realities.

This is the first principle I explained to my friend Mr. Silverberg, the Beverly Hills accountant. I then proceeded to enumerate another principle which by now you are very familiar with—that when you reverse the letters of a Hebrew word, the meaning of the word is often thereby reversed.

With these principles in mind, look more closely at the word for truth, *EMeT*. The first letter is *aleph*, which happens to be the first letter in the alphabet of a total of twenty-seven letters. The second letter in the word is *mem*, the fourteenth letter in the alphabet. That is to say, *mem* falls at the exact midpoint of the alphabet. There are thirteen letters ahead of it and thirteen after it.

The last letter in *EMeT* is *tof*. I asked Mr. Silverberg where he thought *tof* fell in the Hebrew alphabet—given that the first letter is the first in the alphabet, and the middle letter is the middle letter in the alphabet. You can also take a wild guess.

Mr. Silverberg smiled tolerantly at me. He had not become a rich man for nothing. "I would guess that *tof* is the last letter in the Hebrew alphabet." He was exactly right.

We had not yet got around to predicting the Hebrew word for "falsehood." First I wanted to make clear to him that, just as the numbers in spread sheets are not abstract calculations but instead correspond to real life with all its sorrows and joys—here's the amount we spent on Granny's funeral, here's how much we spent on furnishings for the new baby's bedroom—Hebrew letter/numbers also point in a very concrete way to the world around us. In the present case, the letters that designate the word for "truth" tell us important truths about what truth, EMeT, is in the first place.

Confronted with various and conflicting supposedly true accounts of an event, how do you go about determining what the real EMeT is?

FROM BEGINNING TO END

I told Mr. Silverberg that while accountants have unique insights into life that other people come by with greater difficulty, so also do mothers. Every day our seven children confront my wife, Susan, with competing "true" accounts. If one child comes crying to her, saying another child hit her (usually it's a girl fighting with a girl), Susan does what all mothers know instinctively to do in this situation.

First she has the girls tell her the whole story, starting from the very beginning and continuing in sequence, through the middle to the end, leaving nothing out and keeping everything in order.

It usually surfaces that the crying girl who says her sister hit her was not exactly sitting around innocently reading a book when, out of nowhere, up came the other girl and walloped her. More likely the crying girl had first pulled a chair out from under her sister while the latter was preparing to sit down—or some other such hostile act, which was precipitated by some other offense, and so on and so on. These sessions of claim and counterclaim can get very complicated. But if Susan persists, insisting that the girls go in order and leave nothing out from first to last, the truth about the affair is usually ascertainable.

What happens in the discovery of EMeT, then? It is just this: You begin with the aleph, the very beginning. You proceed in order through the middle, the mem. And you don't stop till you reach the end, the tof.

Leave any of these steps out, and you likely will be left with something less than, or even completely different from, the truth.

I enjoy detective stories—Agatha Christie, Sherlock Holmes. Maybe you do, too. Imagine cutting out all the pages in an Agatha Christie novel and putting them together again in an order just slightly different from that intended by the author. If the resulting book were to be reedited and awkward transitions between sentences or paragraphs smoothed out or slightly rewritten, you could produce a story that made superficial sense. But the "truth" revealed at the end of the book— usually the identity of the murderer—would no longer flow logically from what preceded it. In the pursuit of truth, order and sequencing count for a lot. Even the counting itself—from page 1 to page 2 to page 3—is crucial.

Another Hebrew root underscores this point: *samech-peh-resh*, pronounced *SeFeR* when it means "book"; *MiSPaR* when it means "number"; *SoFeR* when it means "scribe" or "counter" (that is, a person who counts). A story, especially a true story of the kind you would find in a book, is thus revealed to be profoundly dependent on numbering or counting: If you change the sequence of pages, or the order of events, the story is converted from true to false. (English has much the same idea in our verb *to tell*. A person *tells* a story in its proper order, and a *teller*, as at a bank, is someone who counts money in sequence. In German, the verb *tell* likewise means both "to tell," as in telling a story, and "to count.")

"Mr. Silverberg," I said, "I have only one more piece of information about Hebrew for you before you can predict the answer. In Hebrew, certain individual letters are eternally stamped with meaning: Some words and ideas are so powerful that no element of them can be part of the opposite word. Truth, EMeT, is considered to be one of the most important foundations of the world. Now I believe you are ready to tell me what the Hebrew word for 'falsehood' is."

(You might want to hum to yourself the theme music from a game show and give it a shot yourself.)

"Well," Mr. Silverberg said, "first of all I'd say that 'falsehood' must be the negation of 'truth.' That might suggest that we reverse the sequence of the letters and begin our hypothetical word with the last letter in the alphabet, *tof*. But, in our case, the last letter of the word *EMeT* is eternally stamped with the concept of truth. That letter has no place in the word that means falsehood.

"So as a second best," continued Mr. Silverberg, "how about kicking off our word with the *second to last* letter of the alphabet. What might that be?"

"That letter would be *shin*," I said, smiling broadly. He'd got it right so far. *Shin* is indeed the first letter in the word we were looking for.

"Now," he said, leaning toward me, "if order and sequence, starting from the beginning and ending at the end, are the key to truth, then falsehood must consist of stopping somewhere before you've reached the end of the matter under investigation. Very likely it consists of only examining one aspect of a story, not even allowing that there is a broad range of information from which to learn." He asked me what the letters are that immediately precede *shin* in the Hebrew alphabet.

"They are [in order] *kuf* and *resh,*" I replied.

Mr. Silverberg reasoned that the Hebrew word for falsehood is composed of the letters *shin-resh-kuf:* the second-to-last letter in the alphabet, followed by the third-to-last, followed by the fourth-to-last. But he hesitated at this spelling. If proper sequencing is a key to getting at the EMeT, then there is too much sequencing in the proposed root, shin-resh-kuf. The root is in exactly reversed sequential order. That couldn't be.

I have to tell you that at this point I was very impressed. Here was an extraordinarily astute man, wise indeed in the ways of numbers. I resolved to fire my then-current accountant and take on Mr. Silverberg instead to help me with financial matters, if I could afford him. (It turned out that I couldn't!)

"So," I said cautiously, "I sense that you are getting ready to give me your educated guess. How are you going to propose that we spell 'falsehood' in Hebrew?"

Mr. Silverberg leaned back in his chair, took a long pull on the cigar he was smoking, and blew the smoke in a gentle draft up to the high ceiling of his study. "Since shin-resh-kuf is too 'sequential' to be right," he said slowly, "but on the other hand since *shin* is very likely the first letter of the word we're seeking, I'm going to place my bet on a spelling that keeps the *shin* in its place at the head of the word but shuffles *resh* and *kuf,* reversing their order. Rabbi Lapin, is the word 'falsehood' in Hebrew spelled shin-kuf-resh?"

Well, of course it is. How could it plausibly be otherwise? The root is pronounced "SHeKeR." In human experience, one might say, SheKeR and EMeT are the ultimate opposites. Truth is truth, no matter how you look at it, and falsehood is falsehood.

I never had an opportunity to tell this wonderful and distinguished man an interesting footnote to the question of EMeT and the meaning of truth. When we say that getting at the truth requires that one pursue the matter in question back to the beginning, to its genesis—back in time as far as the chain of events that led to it will go—this itself begs a question: Once you've started back down that chain, where do you stop?

If my little girl Tamara complains to my wife, Susan, that my other little girl Miriam insulted her, it may turn out that Tamara had antagonized Miriam earlier in the day, leading to the present altercation. But why did Tamara do that? They are both good girls. Perhaps something happened between them a few days earlier. If you wanted to, you could trace a pattern in their relationship, and the relationship between both girls and the rest of the family, between the family and the rest of the world, quite a way backward in time.

NOT REALLY CHAOS

The modern idea proposed by theoretical mathematicians called Chaos Theory is basically a very sophisticated way of saying that nothing in our world started yesterday. Every event is connected to umpteen other events in an impenetrably complex relationship of cause and effect.

A famous illustration of the theory is that of the butterfly flapping its wings in China. Through an indescribably complicated chain of cause and effect, a minuscule change in the atmosphere produces a slightly larger one, which produces a still larger change, and so on—so that the tiny innocent creature could ultimately produce a tornado in Kansas. Chaos Theory is actually the wrong name for this idea, the essence of which is that in the universe there are no random, chaotic events. Everything is linked to everything else. Nothing is without a cause, or rather causes. There is no such thing as "chaos."

As all physicists now agree, the universe is not *infinitely* old. Before a certain moment in history, there was no universe. After that, there was a universe, and then the chain of events began. If we were infinitely wise and knowledgeable, we could trace any given action in our lives, any thought or feeling or whatever, back to that moment before which there was nothing. Some prefer to call that moment the Big Bang. Others call it Genesis.

In theory, then, tracing EMeT back to its very root is possible. In Hebrew the four letters, *yud-kay-vav-kay,* that designate the principle name of God—the ineffable Tetragrammaton—are that root. (Actually the second and third letters are not *kay* but *heh.* Out of respect and awe, Jewish people customarily do not write out the Creator's name, or even spell it as we would any other word.) To put it differently, another name of God is EMeT, Truth. God is the root of all Truth.

THE EMET OF THE MATTER

Tracing events back as far as we can helps us in more practical ways, too. One of the great virtues we can practice in life is gratitude. Sometimes we owe thanks to people who benefited us intentionally. But let us not forget the people who helped us without intending to do so. They deserve our gratitude as well.

The Talmud relates the parable of a man who stepped on a scorpion, which gave him a nasty sting in the foot. The man went down to a river to wash the poison out of his wound. By the riverbank he heard the sound of a little child wailing and coughing. Looking into the rushing current, he saw the child—flapping around helplessly, splashing, gulping, about to drown. The man dived in and saved the child's life.

When the child's father thanked him, the rescuer said, "Don't thank me. Thank the scorpion. If it hadn't stung me I wouldn't have gone down to the river and never would have had the opportunity to save your child."

The scorpion did indeed, however indirectly, save the child's life. That is the EMeT of the matter.

We find the same lesson alluded to in the Bible's book of Exodus. In this story, Moses saves a Jewish man from an Egyptian slave master who is on the verge of beating him to death. Moses slays the Egyptian, and pursued by the authorities, flees into the desert. Soon after, in the land of Midian, he meets some young women drawing water from a well. Some local hoodlums have been menacing the girls, and Moses saves them, too. When the girls get home to their father, they tell him about the Midianite ruffians. He asks who rescued them, and they answer that it was a certain *ish Mitzri*, an Egyptian man.

This is very peculiar. Since when did Moses become an Egyptian? The reason Moses had to escape from Egypt was because he saw himself and acted as a Hebrew, not an Egyptian. The Hebrew Bible, read in the original language, turns out to be full of difficulties like this. Almost every verse is in some way problematic, provoking questions. This is either because the humans who wrote or edited the text were incompetent—which seems unlikely—or some more mysterious Author set out intentionally to provoke our curiosity. Taking the second view, the oral tradition in Judaism supplies answers to all such difficulties.

The answer here is that, when the Midianite girls attribute their salvation to an Egyptian, the reference is not really to Moses but to the Egyptian slave master who cruelly beat the Israelite, prompting the compassionate Moses to save him, which resulted in Moses fleeing into the desert, resulting in Moses saving the girls from their tormentors. Like the scorpion, the slave master deserves some credit here. And that too is the EMeT.

I never got to tell any of this to Mr. Silverberg. For, as I am sad to report, we parted ways much too soon. The times I spent with him, our several sessions of learning about Hebrew and other related matters, were quite memorable and enjoyable. But, as I've shown, he was a very smart man, and in the end he felt that what he'd learned so far was compelling him in a certain direction, toward certain answers to particular questions, toward a certain understanding of ultimate Truth, transcendent EMeT. He realized that if he continued learning, his own sense of honor would compel him to become an observant Jew. As he said to me the last time we met, "Rabbi Lapin, I see where all this is leading, and I don't want to go there." He said so with kindness and, I sensed, a degree of regret.

Why a person, not least someone possessing such a profound intellect, would hesitate to pursue truth to its final destination is an extraordinarily tough question, worthy of a Mr. Silverberg.

CHAPTER TWENTY-TWO

Freedom and the Obligation to Serve

ChoFeSH

חפש

Did you ever feel so burdened by responsibilities that the weight of all the must-dos in your life seemed to press down like an elephant on the back of your neck?

Actually, with a lot of folks the pressure tends to settle in a hot little knot at the base of the spine—the kind of back pain that can only be relieved by a long hot soak in the bathtub. But there's no time for that! You've got to finish that report for the boss, pick the kids up from school, buy the groceries, make a dental appointment, call your parents, get those shoes fixed, drop off the dry cleaning…it just cannot all be done!

Too much to bear? Try the following. Get a large pad of paper and one of those desk calendars, the kind with a little line for every half-hour interval. Now enter all your existing appointments in the calendar, and write down every single thing you have to accomplish on the pad of paper. Be sure to note by when you need to accomplish it and how long it will take. Don't leave anything out. Now go through that list, item by item, and insert each task into an available time slot on your calendar. Are you done? Now don't you feel better?

Try it. It really does work.

Logically, it shouldn't. Having filled your calendar with umpteen niggling appointments, duties, and tasks, you paradoxically feel more relaxed than before, when your calendar was perfectly empty. Anyone looking at your calendar before you began filling it up would think you were the freest person in the world—but in fact you felt crushed. Now you've got every minute packed and suddenly feel unburdened. Almost…free! How can this be? Why does constraining yourself with a tightly packed schedule make you feel *less* burdened?

A principle from the Lord's language will begin to clear up the mystery. A three-letter Hebrew root, spelled backward, almost always produces another meaningful word that in many cases is the exact opposite of the word you started out with. For instance, look at the word *PaRaTZ,* which means "to shatter or spread out." Spelled backward, it is *TzaRaF,* meaning "to bind together"—precisely the opposite of the first meaning.

FAMILY, RIGHTS AND DUTY

What does this have to do with being stressed out and wanting nothing so passionately as to be liberated from the burden you're under? Well, why not examine the Hebrew word that means "free"? It is *ChoFeSH,* spelled *chet-peh-shin.* (The letter *peh* can be pronounced either as a *p* or an *f.*) Reverse the letters of this three-letter root, and you get *shin-peh-chet,* which means "obligation to serve." Let's examine this new root.

One word that's formed from this new, reversed root is *miSH'PaCHah,* or "family." From this we derive an important lesson about the essence of a family. It's a group of people bound together by blood and by love. More critically, it's a group bound by an unbreakable web of mutual obligation to serve one another. The idea of "duty" is as important in the Hebrew Bible as the idea of a "right" is in modern America. Unlike English, Hebrew has no word for the concept of right, as used in children's rights, animal rights, gun-owners' rights, gay rights, right to privacy, right to life, or the myriad other phrases that reflect our growing obsession with rights and our growing indifference to obligations.

In the language of the Bible there are only obligations and duties. No one has a right to life or a right to privacy. But you and I have a *duty* to guard one another's life and respect one another's privacy. Similarly, it's a fine thing to love your family, but love on its own can be a bit vague. It is more valuable in a family to emphasize everyone's obligations and to demand that every member of the family consistently act on them.

The Hebrew word for *family* is based on a concept that seems to be the exact opposite of freedom and indeed is even spelled with the same letters read backwards. A family is the opposite of freedom? That sounds depressing, I know. But it's not. Allow me to explain.

The same three-letter root that produces the word miSH'PaCHah, family, also produces ShiF'Chah, "servant." The opposite of freedom, needless to say, is service. This seems to support the idea that family is a negative, constraining institution. But before we come to that conclusion, let us continue to examine what freedom really means.

I've known people who, looking forward to a well-earned vacation from work, lean back in a chair, gaze contentedly at the ceiling, and exclaim, "I can't wait to get free of that office. I just wish I didn't have to come back after two weeks!" This is very sad—an unfortunate misunderstanding of what it means to be free. We humans do not thrive when we are free of *all* obligations. The best vacations are when we commit ourselves to a new set of obligations: a hiking holiday or perhaps a vacation spent learning a new skill or hobby. We return from this kind of break energized and rejuvenated, eager to return to our work. However, the person who spends his vacation sleeping till noon and then heading to the beach for a strenuous afternoon will return to work at the end of his trip strangely exhausted and dispirited.

THE MEANING OF THE SABBATH

In the Bible, our weekly minivacation is the Sabbath. What happens then? Nothing at all? Wrong! One might be forgiven for thinking that the essence of Sabbath rest, as formulated in the fourth commandment, is to spend the day doing nothing. The Hebrew word for Sabbath, ShaBaT, comes from a root that means "to stop" or "cease." But it would be a mistake to suppose that the Sabbath means we are to do nothing at all.

Each Sabbath I try to cease all *creative* activity. This is to acknowledge that all creativity ultimately stems not from me, a human, but from the Creator, who also ceased His creativity on the Sabbath. Look at the wording of the fourth commandment: "Six days you shall labor and do all your work; but the seventh day is a sabbath of the LORD your God; in it you shall not do any work" (Exodus 20:9–10). The commandment deals not just with the seventh day but also with the entire week. This is a key piece of data.

The essence of Sabbath is not to stop and do nothing—but rather, after spending six days creatively (imitating the Creator), only then to stop. The approach here is holistic. Built into every human being is a kind of spiritual odometer that needs to be reset to zero each week. There is no way we would find the creativity of the workweek fulfilling if we had no regular period of contrast against which our spiritual odometers can measure it.

Think about food. We enjoy dinner much more if we haven't been snacking since lunch. Hunger makes food taste better. No food is more tasteless than *matzoh*, the dry, thin, unleavened cracker Jews eat during the festival of Passover. Many Jews have the custom of not eating this tummy-torturing matzoh for two weeks before the onset of the holiday, and of not eating abundantly for most of the day before the first festival meal when much matzoh will be consumed. The result? By contrast, that first piece of matzoh tastes surprisingly good!

Just so with creative activity. God wants us to imitate Him, to join Him in the work of improving the world through the sweat of our brow. But He knows that if all we do is work, work, work for seven days a week, not only our creativity itself but also our ability to enjoy creativity will suffer as a result. The reverse is also true: A person who turns sixty-five and retires with plans to do no more than sit in a rocking chair technically cannot observe the Sabbath. For seven days a week he abstains from creativity, so the seventh day for him becomes just another day of doing nothing.

So doing just plain *nothing* is not what Sabbath observance is all about. Doing nothing is actually depressing and frustrating. Take a look at another example: why many people find art museums tiring. A piece of art, such as a painting, is intended to stir your soul, and the best art does just that. But in a museum picture after picture is presented to you. Though you walk about the gallery on your own power, your role is basically passive. All you are doing is looking and sometimes listening. Since you are engaged in nothing really creative, you are reduced to an object. And being an object is very boring.

It is more exciting to view only a few pieces, taking the time to analyze, compare, and learn about them, rather than force yourself to see each and every piece on display. Invariably, children brought to a museum who have learned something about the artist, the times in which he lived, and what to look for in his paintings will find the experience much more interesting than if they have not done their advance work. In this way the art viewer becomes a participant rather than merely an observer.

THE JOY OF PREPARATION

We humans are programmed to find enjoyment and stimulation only when we've worked for it. The truth is that we only appreciate freedom—the freedom of a Sabbath or of a vacation—in the context of the effort that makes it possible. It's actually a mistake to think that a Jewish Sabbath *really* begins at sundown the previous evening. In reality, a Jewish family commences Sabbath preparation as soon as the previous Sabbath is over. This preparation takes two forms. The first is by being as creative as possible over the first six days of the week. In addition, any delicacy that is found during the week is tucked away to enjoy on the following Sabbath.

When Jewish women light Shabbat candles at sundown on Friday, the warm glow of the candles signals the successful completion of all the work they did to make the blessing of Shabbat possible. At the end of the Sabbath, Saturday, Jews signal the day's completion by holding up a cup of wine. The cup must literally overflow its rim, a symbol of anticipation of the week of overflowing creativity we look forward to, as we launch immediately into preparing for the *next* Sabbath.

I've had some experience with long-term preparation, which makes this idea especially meaningful to me. My family has a tradition of taking boating trips for a month or so each summer. The children are already hearty sailors. Our running joke is that even the younger kids have squeezed more saltwater out of their socks than most adults do in a lifetime. They enjoy running the boat and doing the navigation. But fully half the fun is getting ready for the trip.

When you sail across an ocean, failing to prepare can be a big problem. One summer we set out to sail from Los Angeles to Hawaii. Some goodly distance across the Pacific, I decided to check on the amount of freshwater in stock. Unfortunately, I happened to be more exhausted than I realized and with bleary eyes, I stuck a dip stick into the freshwater tank and brought it out. To my horror and astonishment, I saw that the tank was empty.

It was my worst nightmare come true, as we did not expect landfall for several days. I imagined consoling my little children with whatever moisture could be drained from cans of stored fruit and vegetables. *Here, darling, I'm sorry you're thirsty. Have some tuna juice.* Later, when I was a little more rested, I tried the dip stick again. Thank God! Somehow, through my weariness, I had misread it the first time. In fact, the freshwater tank was full.

This harrowing experience gave me an appreciation for preparation. Getting ready for a major trip or event is certainly stressful, but the consequences of failing to prepare are ever more so. I can testify that nothing about the trip drew my family closer together than the need to make sure that absolutely everything we needed was ready and onboard before we set sail.

Yet I can also tell you that few activities convey the same sense of freedom as sailing across an ocean. So we begin to see the glimmer of a resolution to the mystery of why CHoFeSH (freedom) is the opposite of MiSH'PaCHaH (family)-SHiF'CHaH (servant). You see, the English language fails to adequately distinguish between good freedom and bad freedom. Freedom from all obligations is a terrible form of freedom. It might better be translated as "license."

In Hebrew, the word ChoFeSH has no place in a family. Real freedom, the good kind, is what we experience when we have selected our obligations and are performing them. It is a deep and joyful sense of freedom utterly undiminished by the nagging guilt that often accompanies the bad freedom. Every schoolchild knows the difference between an evening spent watching television before the homework is completed and the same evening once all homework obligations are discharged.

The ancient rabbis of the Talmud hint at the same idea when they direct our attention to another important Hebrew word, *CHaRuT*, which means both "engraved" and "free" but only alludes to the good kind of freedom. The context here is a discussion of the Ten Commandments, which the Bible tells us were "engraved" on two stone tablets. What the wise old rabbis meant is that freedom is somehow the same thing as being engraved. This may sound strange, but it is really quite clear and rather valuable to know and incorporate into our lives.

You've heard the expression "It's not written in stone," meaning that whatever is being discussed—a date, a time, an obligation, a duty—is not absolutely necessary or obligatory. Idiomatically, "cast in concrete" means the same thing. In other words, putting the Talmud's somewhat cryptic statement as clearly as possible, we are most truly free when our lives are engraved, written in stone, or cast in concrete. It is telling us that, paradoxically, the Ten Commandments, although "engraved in stone," really have the capacity to liberate us and bestow the good kind of freedom upon us. It is as if knowing where the boundaries are really frees us. Children often demonstrate this to us in how more relaxed they seem to be with parents who clearly delineate the boundaries of acceptable behavior.

Sound crazy? I hope not. Remember how you felt after you wrote out all your tasks on an hour-by-hour desk calendar? You felt a lot freer than you did when your calendar was empty.

IMPRISONMENT

As I've already shared, I served a synagogue on the boardwalk in Venice, California, for fifteen years. Venice was, and I believe still is, a rather countercultural sort of place. To that beach came young and old in search of freedom—the bad kind of freedom, the kind with no obligations. Those seekers of Shangri-La slept till noon on the park benches, drank beer on the sidewalks, played drums and guitars if they felt like it, and indulged in strange and prohibited substances. No homes, no jobs. Quite free!

Not exactly. These same individuals had no money, no transportation, no medical care—none of the advantages that allow those of us with more settled lives to fully pursue our ambitions and enjoy the Creator's world. Basically, they were stuck there on Venice beach—a very attractive setting on which to be imprisoned but trapped nevertheless. Do you remember that old song with the line, "Freedom's just another word for nothing left to lose…" Wrong! Having nothing left to lose is like living in a particularly painful prison.

Compare the situation of Venice beach vagrants with that of a typical husband or wife who might have attended my synagogue right there facing the famous Pacific Ocean sunsets. A family man is restrained, one might say, by his family—obliged, engraved, his life cast in concrete. Yet he is also surrounded by a cocoon of love and support, which he receives every day from his wife and children. He is inspired and driven by the sheer privilege and exhilaration of being their provider. He is immune to the desperation and hopelessness that is the legitimate legacy of those free-living denizens of Venice beach. The good kind of freedom, cherut, comes through service and self-restraint. The bad kind of freedom, ChoFeSH, is the opposite of family and genuine service.

We can apply this lesson practically in areas of our lives well beyond the Sabbath, beyond vacations, even beyond the unfortunate concept of mandatory retirement at age sixty-five. All we have to do is treat each day with all its myriad of tasks as another thrilling opportunity to pursue freedom—the good kind of freedom, of course. I mean the kind of freedom that springs from an obligation undertaken and well done.

How about those of us who occasionally feel a little depressed and bored? Why not take this as an indication that it is time to undertake some new obligations? Perhaps some volunteer service to improve your neighborhood and community. Maybe a way in which to make yourself invaluable to some other person or family. As my father, who was also my teacher, used to say, there is only one thing worse than having too much to do: Not having enough to do.

Now, start making that list.…

PART SIX

SPIRITUAL LIFE

CHAPTER TWENTY-THREE

Ascend to the Heights

PaLeiL
פלל

S ome people find that praying comes naturally to them, but for me this certainly is not true. Praying is not something I related to instinctively when I was growing up. In retrospect, I am not embarrassed about this; after all, I did not grow up naturally able to dive off the high board or cook an omelette either. I had to be taught these things, as well as be receptive to learning them, and when I was young it just didn't happen.

At one point I thought that I understood heartfelt prayer. My good friend Aubrey was an accomplished climber who always radiated such joy about his sport that I envied his passion for sunrises at the summit. "Come with me," he invited. So I did. It was not too long after beginning our ascent began that I developed a newfound fervor for prayer. Have you ever heard people say that there are no atheists in foxholes? Well, I have news for you. I don't think there are too many atheists among those who dangle off cliffs from slender nylon ropes either. I desperately proposed a deal to God: *You get me through this safely, and I will never ever attempt to climb a mountain again!*

Eventually we reached the summit. It was breathtakingly beautiful, but not as beautiful as the valley below looked to me once we returned there. I lay on my back in the long fragrant grass, gazed up at the peak from which we had just descended, and felt humiliated by the realization that what I had been doing up there was not praying, it was simply begging.

Begging depresses the spirit. If your outstretched palm is ignored, you feel rejected. If a quarter is dropped into your hand by the pedestrian walking by with averted eyes, you feel humiliated. So if what I had been doing on the crags up above the clouds was begging, then what was praying? I had been taught how to dress and how to drive. I had been taught how to eat in polite company and how to fly a small plane. But nobody had ever managed to teach me how to pray.

Perhaps because praying deeply and meaningfully seemed second nature to my parents, they weren't able to relate to my difficulties. I imagine it would have been similarly challenging for the great composer Bach if one of his sons had been unmoved by the grandeur of music. I felt baffled watching my father swing through his morning prayers with ease. I could say the words, but the act did nothing for me. I felt no sensation other than a vague self-consciousness. It was like watching someone juggle: I wanted to ask, "How do you do that?"

It was not until years later, as an adult, that I did ask how to pray and, not surprisingly, the answer lay in the Hebrew word for prayer. It had been in front of me all along. The word is *PaLeiL,* or in actual usage as in "I pray," *ani (I) MiTPaLeiL.* Verbs tend to convey meaning with great precision in the Lord's language. Some verbs are what we call reflexive, meaning that the actions are things you do to yourself; this verb is one of those. These verbs usually start off with the prefix *MiT* in the present tense. For instance, I dress myself—*ani (I) MiTLaBeiSH.*

Now why on earth would the verb meaning "I pray" exist only in the reflexive form, as if to say that praying is something I do to myself? I had assumed praying was something we did to God, as it were. How very peculiar.

RECONCILING TWO IMAGES

Now we must turn to the meaning of the root of the word. By carefully examining the context in which the word is used biblically, PaLeiL means "to judge" or "to reconcile." Judging and reconciling are really the same idea. Each entails taking two apparently incompatible realities and blending them into a unified outcome. You now have all the information necessary to grasp the meaning of prayer. It means looking at yourself as you see you, and then looking at yourself as God sees you. It means flipping between these two apparently incompatible images of you and attempting to reconcile them with one another. It means, in other words, trying to judge yourself.

But wait! What does this have to do with talking to God? Take it easy—we are not there yet. You didn't think we could dismantle the details of one of humanity's most complex activities in just a paragraph or two, did you? This will take at least another couple of paragraphs, so hang on!

So far we have deduced that the launching pad for prayer is looking into ourselves and contrasting what we see with what we imagine God sees when He looks into our souls. In other words, we judge ourselves. Does this create a tension? Yes? Excellent, we are making progress. Now flip backward and forward as rapidly as you can between these two seemingly irreconcilable images. You remember that old-fashioned children's toy, a piece of wood that can be whirled around a central handle. On one side of the wooden paddle is the picture of a soldier with his arm raised while the other side depicts the identical soldier with his arm lowered. Spin the paddle around at just the right speed and what do you see? Instead of two seemingly different and irreconcilable pictures, you now see a soldier waving his arm at you.

BEAMING MESSAGES TO GOD

Okay, so you now have this procedure of rapidly flipping between a right-eye view and a left-eye view of yourself. This oscillation converts what appeared to be two different views into a sort of three-dimensional moral picture of yourself. But how can this exercise beam a message directly to God?

Think of how a radio signal is launched into space. You have heard of the term *frequency*. For instance, your favorite talk show might be found on the AM band at a frequency of say, 1300 kilocycles. This means the station broadcasts a signal that fluctuates backward and forward 1,300,000 times each second. If you are listening to music on the FM band, you might be tuned to a station that broadcasts a signal that fluctuates 90 million times each second. It doesn't much matter. All that matters is that the only way to make a signal jump off a piece of wire we call the antenna and travel through space is to make that signal oscillate or fluctuate between two apparent opposites. In radio technology we might refer to those two polar opposites as positive and negative.

The resemblance to prayer technology is startling. We must train our minds to fluctuate between two images of ourselves. They are polar opposites. One is how God might see us, while the other is how we see ourselves. Indeed, we could quite reasonably refer to those two images as the positive and the negative views of ourselves. Just as fluctuating between positive and negative causes a radio signal to leap off the wire and beam away into space, fluctuating between these positive and negative images causes a prayer signal, as it were, to leap off our beings and beam away toward God.

Far-fetched? Not at all. Think of how the cowboy cracks his whip to produce that sound small boys find quite irresistible. By flicking his wrist, he sends an oscillation down the whip, a sort of up-down wave shape. Only when the tip of the whip bends back on itself do the oscillations produce a loud report that leaps off the whip and begins the journey to our ears.

We still have a problem. We may well have explained how we are able to project out some sort of spiritual signal. But how do we superimpose upon that signal the things we wish to talk to God about? The radio analogy can help us still further. I mentioned the AM and FM bands, which you can see on the dial of your radio. They stand for Amplitude Modulation and Frequency Modulation. These are two different technologies for superimposing the words of your favorite talk show host or your favorite music onto the underlying carrier wave. The basic oscillation or fluctuation allows the signal to jump off the wire antenna. By itself, it contains no intelligible data such as voice or music; it is just a carrier wave. The intelligible information needs to be superimposed upon the carrier. Well, in prayer the same is true. Once we have succeeded in escaping our self-centered nature and have produced a "prayer signal" that projects outward from ourselves, we must now superimpose what we want to say onto that carrier wave.

That is what distinguishes prayer from begging. Begging is an act of self-centeredness: I have a need so I am asking you to take care of my need. You are only a facilitator for what I want. Unlike begging, prayer requires us to find a way to emerge from our self-centeredness. The best way to do so is to focus on what we each look like from the outside looking in. By reconciling God's view of us with our own self-image, we judge ourselves more dispassionately. Then—and only then—are we ready to superimpose our own communication with God.

There is just one more point of clarification. There is no meaning to judgment if the system under which I am being judged is capricious. Anytime someone uses terms like *good, bad, moral,* or *immoral,* we ought to demand to know according to what system they make those judgments. This is why praying without God is meaningless. We can only pray to a God who has expectations of us. Without those expectations we cannot hope to create a tension between how we view ourselves and how God sees us. And it is precisely the tension between those two polar opposites that makes prayer possible.

You have certainly heard of the fellow who cried that he had prayed to God for a Ferrari but God ignored him. The wise man listening then tapped him on the shoulder. "Excuse me," he politely said, "God did not ignore you. He listened to your prayer and then He said no." History does not record how the European-car enthusiast responded. But there is one thing we do know. Prayer is more than simply tacking a list of requests on to that carrier wave we beam out by flipping between the images. In reality, we are asking God to help us diminish the contrast between the two images so as to become as worthy as possible of the benefits we request.

Clearly there is a painfully large chasm between how I view myself and how God views me. This I know because I fully understand the system by which God judges, and I also know His expectations for me. He may not expect me to be as great as Moses, but He certainly wants Daniel Lapin to achieve whatever greatness Daniel Lapin can possibly achieve. We are further asking for the ability and wisdom to accept a no to requests that are far less frivolous than a Ferrari, in full understanding that God knows best. Once I was taught these principles and techniques, I became a little better at praying. I also was better able to understand the effectiveness of prayer.

ESCAPE THE LIMITATIONS OF SELF-CENTEREDNESS

According to the ancient rabbis, another key principle of prayer is that when I pray for someone else's need, if I have a similar need my prayers are answered with greater dispatch. You see, very few beggars beg on behalf of other needy people. They tend to be self-centered. Prayer is one of the wonderful tools a benevolent God has made available for people to communicate with Him and thereby to escape the limitations of their own self-centeredness.

We know from famous medical studies, some of which have been conducted by doctors who do not believe in God, that prayer helps in the recovery of the ill. Remarkably, prayer is effective not only when the patient is aware of prayers being said on his behalf; prayer also helps even when the patient is oblivious of anyone praying for his recovery.

Communicating with God through prayer is one of the most exciting adventures imaginable. I no longer feel stupid for having taken so long to learn how to do it. I am only grateful that, unlike so many other skills still hidden from me, prayer has become accessible. We still do not know the full extent of prayer's power, but only those who practice the skill regularly will stand any chance of finding out. I may not climb mountains anymore, but through the magic of prayer, I can ascend great heights just the same. And so can you.

CHAPTER TWENTY-FOUR

The Inner Joy of Overcoming Limits

MaKOM

מקום

S ome people blame the crash of the Hindenburg for altering the course of twentieth-century travel. They argue that when the great German airship crashed and burned in New Jersey in 1939, it not only demolished the Zeppelin company's prospects, but it frightened people away from that mode of flight. If so, this was a pity. Travel on a large dirigible was so much more comfortable than flying is today. Instead of being sealed into a narrow aluminum cylinder and hurtled across the country, airship travelers enjoyed sleeping cabins, dining rooms, observation windows, and other comfortable amenities during their journeys. I suspect, however, that the airship was doomed anyway.

For most of the twentieth century, great ocean liners sped across the Atlantic. In three days or so, they conveyed comfortable and cosseted passengers between London and New York. But the possibility of covering that distance in six hours on an airplane doomed the ocean liners. In spite of the memorable cuisine and ornate surroundings that the trans-Atlantic voyage promised, passengers preferred speed to comfort when it came to "crossing the pond." This preference continues today. There is no shortage of Concorde travelers willing to spend astronomical sums and endure claustrophobically cramped conditions in order to go from New York to London within three hours on a supersonic airliner.

This assures me that it is wrong to blame the Hindenburg crash for dooming the age of airships. Those regal blimps were goners long before that fateful disaster. In the futile quest to achieve instantaneous transport, humans would have eventually rejected the sixteen-hour airship crossing just as they rejected the three-day ocean liner crossing once a faster alternative was available. It is only the rarity and expense of supersonic transport that maintains the viability of conventional air travel. People would have abandoned airships just as they abandoned ocean liners and indeed, even railway travel.

Just think of how few contemporary Americans have relished the delights of a train journey across our beautiful land. Now that it is not more expensive to fly from Los Angeles to Washington, D.C., in an airplane than it is to make the same journey more slowly in a railway carriage, we have abandoned railway travel in droves. Although that train is spacious and luxurious, people seem to prefer a crowded, uncomfortable airplane. How do we explain our feverish quest to save time? Why do we all appear to be consumed by a desperate desire to get there faster? Why do we not delight more in the journey than in the arriving?

BEING TWO PLACES AT ONCE

Answering these questions is a lot easier when we examine Hebrew's word for "space" or "place": MaKOM. Another way of asking those questions is questioning how consumed we seem to be with shrinking space or place. We strive to come as close as possible to being in two places at almost the same time. In other words, quite subconsciously, we are trying to achieve omnipresence. When we risk a ticket by speeding through traffic, we are expressing our inner frustration that we simply cannot be in two places at the same time.

It seems to be a stubborn and frustrating fact of human existence that we simply cannot be everywhere at once. But that, of course, is not true of God. And this is exactly the divine quality we describe when little children question us about the Almighty. They struggle to understand how God can be here to listen to our bedtime prayers while He is simultaneously over at little Jimmy's house to hear his prayers. He is everywhere at once, we explain.

It is odd that we seem so driven to emulate God in this particular divine attribute. We seem frustrated by our inability to be in more than one place at a time. Not surprisingly, MaKOM is the Hebrew word that not only means space or place, but it is also one of the words used to describe God. Whenever we need to discuss God with particular emphasis upon His ability to be everywhere at once—His ability to be omnipresent—we can use the word MaKOM.

OUR CURRENT LOVE AFFAIR

Transport is not the only way in which we seek to overcome the frustrating human limitation of being in only place at a time. We are in the midst of a love affair with telephones, radio, television, and yes, even the Internet.

Do you recall the seductiveness of those old walky-talky radios? Or how about the old citizens' band transceivers? Now it is cell phones. These technological marvels appeal to us because, on some level, they allow us to escape that frustrating limitation of space, allowing us to talk to someone far off as if we were in the same room. All these electronic breakthroughs allow us to sprawl in our favorite living room chair while enjoying the feeling that we are not merely somewhere else, but actually everywhere else. We can chat on the phone with our daughter in Baltimore while watching some of our fellow citizens chasing a ball in a Dallas stadium.

For humans, feeling godlike is enormously pleasurable. Two cell phones? Sure, why not? Multilined cell phones? Of course. Cell phones with miniature screens that connect me to the limitless vistas of Web surfing? Please, when can I get one? Seven hundred cable channels on my television that allow me to vicariously participate in the exciting lives of thousands of other people all over the world? Sign me up! They all offer some reprieve from the horrible frustration of being human instead of God, of being condemned to being in only one place at a time.

All this becomes clear from realizing the implications of having a name for God that means "everywhere." We can understand that our desire to be everywhere at once, our desire to escape the limits of our own bodies, is nothing other than our desire to become godlike or at one with God.

Any great book that makes you utterly forget time while it escorts your soul on a soaring adventure of discovery is taking you outside of your body's limits. After reading for a while, you finally return to reality with a start and look at your watch, incredulous at how much time had passed. Where were you? It was almost like an out-of-body experience. You found it a satisfying interlude, partially because it made you less material—godlier. You were operating in the spiritual and intangible sphere of those thoughts and ideas that leapt off the page and into your brain. Where were you? In a sense, you were everywhere. Exactly like God.

NUMERICAL INSIGHT

MaKOM is made up of the four Hebrew letters *M, K, O,* and *M.* From the table of numerical equivalents, the word's numerical value is:

$$40+100+6+40=186.$$

Store in your memory the fact that the numerical equivalent of God's omnipresence, or being everywhere, is 186. You should also be aware that the basic and most frequently used name of God in the Bible is made up of these letters: *Y, H, V, H;* with the following numerical equivalents: 10, 5, 6, 5. What do these four numbers have to do with 186? Watch!

How do we convert length measurements such as inches, feet, yards, or miles into area or space measurements? We square them, arriving at area measurements such as square inches, square feet, square yards, and square miles. For instance, let us imagine that we owned a small rectangular field. One edge, the long edge, measures twelve yards while the other, the breadth, is found to be four yards long. Let us say we need to know how many corn plants we can sow. Well, the seed package informs us that corn can be planted at a density of, say, ten stalks every square yard. How do we discover how many square yards we have available? The area or the space available in our field for planting corn would be forty-eight square yards. We multiplied the length of one edge by the length of the other edge. Twelve multiplied by four yielded the correct answer of forty-eight.

Imagine now that the numbers 10, 5, 6, and 5 represent the four-letter, linear name for God. This is similar to saying that one edge of the "God field" measures 10, 5, 6, 5. Since God is God, the other edge also measures 10, 5, 6, and 5. This God field is a square with both length and breadth measuring the same. Now, how might we obtain the area or space value of the God field? Why, it is simply the same process we used in the earlier example of the little cornfield. One edge is:

	10, 5, 6, 5
The other edge is	10, 5, 6, 5

Multiplying, we get: 100, 25, 36, 25

Add them all together like this:

$$100 + 25 + 36 + 25 = 186.$$

You will of course remember that the numerical equivalent of God's attribute of omnipresence, or being everywhere, is 186, the numerical value of one of His names, MaKOM. In other words, if 10, 5, 6, and 5 (Y W V H) represents the straight line depiction of God, as it were, then the spatial or omnipresent depiction of God must be God squared, or 186—or, of course, MaKOM.

IMITATING GOD

One way to be godlike is to imitate God, and that is precisely what many of us try to do. For instance, when confronted with a moral dilemma, wise people ask themselves what would God want them to do. But even unreligious folk find themselves attracted to the godlike feeling that can come from overcoming human limitations. Every time we strive to push beyond where we previously thought we were stuck, we feel exhilarated. Athletes, business professionals, housewives, and everyone else all experience the "high" that comes from pushing just a little harder. This sense of exhilaration we feel is nothing other than our souls exulting in the tiny triumph of becoming just a bit more godlike. We are thrilled to feel just a little less limited and restricted. To some extent, this exhilaration can be experienced in different ways. Some sense it by running a mile in four minutes, others by increasing sales targets, or by building a large and successful business. Less thrillingly, you could feel it in a passive way by watching television or listening to the radio. Anything that takes you beyond and outside of yourself will do it.

One of the most thrilling ways to emulate God, however, is to overcome a moral challenge. Trying to be a little better than we were yesterday, or struggling to be a little more compassionate, a little more thoughtful and considerate, a little more disciplined than we had been, is just plain fun.

On the other hand, chasing over the globe, constantly buying the latest technological means of communication, escaping the limitations of being human through movies and even too frequently through books, can be wearying. In contrast, when we imitate God by expanding our souls—for example, by battling and overcoming a character deficiency—we can feel an even greater high than an athlete enjoys after a strenuous and satisfying physical workout. The desire to imitate God is planted in us; how we achieve that goal defines us.

Parents are blessed with the opportunity to grow through interaction with their children each day. Friends can practice growth within their relationships. Work provides most of us with other opportunities to reach beyond our limits. The trick is to awake to each new morning reveling in the wealth of opportunities the day will provide for us to experience the inner joy of escaping limits. Of course we are going to rush around trying to save time. Of course we will feel dismay at numerous frustrating delays. But through it all, we can remain happy by remembering that it all springs from our powerful, subconscious urge to emulate God by trying to be everywhere and trying to do everything all at once. If we can harness that urge more thoughtfully by using it to expand our awareness and love for God and one another, we will have discovered the joy of truly overcoming our human limits. It may not be possible to fully achieve, but it is really fun to try.

CHAPTER TWENTY-FIVE

The Source of Spiritual Energy

B'RaCHa

ברכ(ה)

L et's pretend to be screenwriters.

The scene: *A modern traveler hurtles back in his time machine to a primitive and remote village.*

The action: *The time traveler is captured by fierce-looking warriors* (I could get into this) *who roughly drag him to the hut of the chief who is well known for his cannibalistic tendencies.* (Do you think that is laying it on a bit too thick?) *Eager to escape his desperate plight, our hero extracts a flask from his pocket and pours what appears to be water around the feared chief's hut. As his tormentors watch the futile antics of their helpless captive, he takes a cigarette lighter from his pocket and ignites the liquid. The hut erupts in flames and is completely destroyed within minutes. Our hero escapes the burning hut in which the chief is being roasted, and the amazed villagers immediately appoint him their new chief.*

That is as far as I can go with the story for now.

Time travel is a popular plot that we find both in books and in movies. From his ordinary suburban surroundings, our hero finds himself thrust back to an earlier age. Because of the things he knows and the things he can do, the locals of the day assume he possesses magical powers.

In our story, our intrepid traveler has proven himself to the villagers to be more powerful than their chief ever was. After all, with only a flick of his wrist he destroyed a powerful chief along with his hut. Yet from *our* vantage point we know that our voyager is actually a rather ordinary sort of fellow with no special powers.

He caused all the impressive damage simply by using the highly concentrated energy stored in gasoline. It was not his own power that caused the hut to vanish in flames, but rather his ability to harness the energy that had long ago been captured within the chemical makeup of petroleum. In modern times, that substance was extracted by a petroleum company and made available to customers. Within gasoline was wonderful molecular magic—great quantities of potential energy that had been, originally, the gift of the sun.

Our adventurer possessed no magical powers; he simply unleashed a source of energy. He did not put the energy there in the first place; neither did he even understand the complex chemistry involved. He simply knew the rules of using that energy—light it and it burns.

There are other wonderful sources of energy in our world. We may not understand the complexities of their origins but as long as we know how to use them, we can all benefit from them.

I tell this story because it helps us to understand the mysterious power of a blessing; what in Hebrew is called a *B'RaCHa*.

DEPLOYING ANCIENT TRIGGERS

The ancient rabbis insisted that we should never despise a blessing. That would seem to be obvious. I am sure we could all benefit from blessings. But the rabbis had more to say. They added that we should greatly appreciate a blessing regardless of how very ordinary the person offering it may be. Even a fool offering us a blessing is bestowing something of great value.

This would suggest that the power of a blessing has little to do with the qualities of the individual delivering it—the one igniting the gasoline, as it were. It is not only famous sages or holy saints who can bless others to wonderful effect. Sometimes even ordinary folk like you and me can do so, too. This is because if we do it right, when we bless another person—much like our time-traveling hero—we can deploy or trigger an ancient power much greater than ourselves.

Insights into the Hebrew language have been handed down through the millennia by Jewish tradition. Analyzing the Hebrew word B'RaCHa lets us understand what a B'RaCHa or blessing really is. Let us look closely at this word and observe an interesting peculiarity.

B'RaCHa is composed of three letters, *bet-resh-chof,* that share a common factor. In gematria, the aspect of biblical teaching that deals with extracting meaning from

Hebrew words by calculating their numerical equivalents, these letters are assigned the following values: *bet* stands for the number 2, *resh* is 200, and *chof* is 20.

Now these letters, which spell the word B'RaCHa, happen to be unique, for they are the only letters in the whole Hebrew alphabet whose number equivalent is exactly double the number equivalent of the letter immediately preceding it. The value of *bet*, 2, is twice that of the preceding letter *aleph*, or 1. *Resh*, 200, follows *kuf*, 100. And *chof*, 20, follows *yud*, or 10 in the sequence of alphabetical letters.

While no scholar of French, English, or German would bother to make such an observation about those languages, Hebrew is unique. As I've already observed, the Lord's language is as much a mathematical code as it is a form of conventional linguistic communication. Recognizing that the three letters that compose the word for B'RaCHa are the only three letters whose numerical value is exactly double the letters preceding them tells us that a blessing has something to do with *doubling*. For confirmation take a look at some of the other words formed from the same three-letter root, albeit with the letters appearing in different order. Each one has a meaning that alludes to the "doubling" or "twoness" reflected in the letters themselves. Here are some words formed by mixing up and rearranging the letters *bet, resh,* and *chof.*

B'CHoR: This word means "firstborn," and the firstborn enjoys one famous distinction. In biblical law, the firstborn boy in a family is entitled to a share of inheritance exactly double that of the other children.

CHeRuV: Cherub, a kind of angel. (Remember that the alphabet's second letter, *bet,* can sound like a *b* or a *v*.) The most famous cherubs in the Bible are those that surmount the ark of the covenant, which resided in the Holy of Holies of the Temple in Jerusalem. There were, of course, *two* of them.

Interestingly, the Talmud relates that these cherubs functioned as a type of spiritual barometer measuring the level of closeness between the Creator and the Jewish people. When the Israelite nation was in close communion with Him, the cherubs faced each other across the top of the ark. In periods of alienation from Him, the cherubs pivoted and faced away from each other. When Jerusalem was conquered and the Temple sacked by the Roman Empire in A.D. 70, triumphant Roman soldiers entered the Temple and carried off the ark. The ordinary Jews in the streets of the holy city were overcome by depression until they saw the ark as it was carried past them in procession: The cherubs, they noticed, not only faced each other but were locked in the closest possible embrace.

RaCHaV: To ride. Though this word may be a little less obvious, upon reflection we can see that "riding" is a doubling activity for it can be done only by the interaction of two entities, namely the rider and that which is ridden be it horse, motorcycle, or any other combination.

And finally, *miCH'BaR:* Cover. The idea here is much the same as with RaCHaV. When you "cover" something, there is again a necessary twoness: the covered object and the cover itself. Imagine the waiter at an elegant restaurant serving with a great flourish the roast duck you ordered. Out he comes with an outsized silver dish, held aloft on his right hand, but the bird itself is invisible until he removes the shining, silvery, dome-shaped cover surmounting the dish. The cover is as much a part of the show as the food it covers.

In B'RaCHa we likewise find that a blessing wraps up a requisite twoness. Every blessing diminishes the self-centeredness that can trap us in the prison of ego and oneness. If a blessing does nothing more than lead us to acknowledge God as the source of all blessing, we have already escaped the pain of seeing ourselves as the only entity of significance. But it usually does far more. It links us in a powerful embrace not only to other people but also to the very world around us. Merely uttering a blessing emphasizes the reality of me and something or someone else. When I express a blessing, I am acknowledging that the "me" is not all there is.

The word B'RaCHa has another grammatical message imbedded in it. B'RaCHa is a feminine word. In Hebrew, as in Spanish, French, and other Romance languages, nouns can be either masculine or feminine. Consequently, verbs and adjectives are modified slightly depending on whether they are being used in conjunction with a masculine or feminine noun. While the Frenchman may not understand why he says "La Benediction" rather than "Le Benediction," the Hebrew aficionado finds a lesson here—because Hebrew is a language without coincidences. Every fact about a word is significant and subject to explanation. So too here. If a blessing is feminine in its linguistic form, we need to know the reason.

THE ABILITY TO REPRODUCE

One of the most inescapable realities of being a woman is the ability to give birth. While some small physical material from the man is needed, it is a woman's body that forms and nurtures a growing baby and from which the baby emerges. There is a natural connection between mother and child. Her body is the one that sustained the growing baby and can even continue to do so after birth by supplying milk for the infant. It is her hormones that intimately react to each phase of the baby's development and birth. In her ability to reproduce, she shares something in common with every feminine Hebrew word like B'RaCHa.

What do I mean? Well, this idea occurred to me late one night when my car ran out of gas on a lonely road. The infrequent passing driver barely saw me as he sped by. I was alone and assumed that I'd have to wait till morning to flag down a passing car. As I sat in the driver's seat for a couple of hours, on the verge of dozing off, a car approached from behind and stopped. I saw the headlights go out and watched as a trio of somewhat rough-looking characters emerged from the car.

I braced myself when the men tapped on my window, but their faces announced no menacing intent. In fact, they very kindly offered to fill my tank with enough gas to reach the next town. When I asked them how I could possibly repay them for this kindness and began to take out my wallet, they gently refused. "Don't worry about it," said one. "When you get to the next gas station, just buy yourself a gas canister and keep it in your trunk. That way, if you ever come upon some other guy who ran out of gas on a road like this, you can help him like we helped you."

And that was exactly what I did. Whenever those I helped would ask how they could repay me, I gave the same answer I heard from my three benefactors on that dark, lonely night. You might say that their blessing to me was reproduced over and over again. A blessing has the capacity to reproduce and create new blessings. Will every blessing reproduce? No, of course not. Not every woman gives birth, either. However, a woman has the ability to reproduce and so does a blessing.

One finds an analogy in the natural world. Scientists have formulated what is called the Laws of Conservation of Matter and Energy. In the physical world, matter and energy can convert into one another, and they are eternal. For example, when you burn a candle, the quantity of wax that melts doesn't cease to exist; it turns into fumes as well as into energy in the form of light and heat. Blessings are like that too. They never die. God blessed the seventh day and called it His Sabbath, a fact that Jews acknowledge by saying a blessing over a special glass of wine each Friday night. God's blessing didn't simply expire at the conclusion of that first Sabbath. The Sabbath never uses up its share of blessing. The offspring of that original divine blessing continue to bless each human who steps under the shelter of the Sabbath each week.

A B'RaCHa is about continuity. This is why one of the most conspicuous examples of a regular blessing is the one religious Jewish parents bestow upon their children each week as the Sabbath is about to commence. Children are the key to our continuity. They confer immortality upon us just as we do for our parents and grandparents. Through our children maintaining the values that shape our lives, we in a sense continue to live here on earth through them. If they reproduce and are blessed with their own children, in whom they inculcate the very same values, then in a sense we never die.

STAYING GROUNDED

We now arrive at the next clue contained in the Hebrew word for blessing: The word for blessing is the same as the word for knee. Insignificantly, the vowels are slightly different, giving us *BeReCH*; however, the root *bet-resh-chof* means both blessing and knee.

If, like me, you've occasionally hurt your knees by running in insufficiently cushioned running shoes, you know how essential a part of the body your knees really are. Without knees, there are basically three things you can't do: You can't reach down to touch the ground. You can't run. And you can't jump. Your knees allow you to do all these things; metaphorically speaking, so does a blessing.

Try touching the ground without bending your knees. Yes, if you are extraordinarily lithe, it can be done. For most of us, however, touching the ground without knees would mean hurling ourselves to the floor and falling flat on our back or face, but that's no fun. Much better just to bend our knees and *kneel*.

Kneeling, of course, just happens to be the classic pose most associated with prayer. Many of us who worship will find ourselves on our knees from time to time. For Jews, kneeling is so important that it constitutes a crucial aspect of the Yom Kippur service on the Day of Atonement. In America it is not uncommon when petitioning God to fall on one's knees and ask for His blessing—a custom derived from the worship service in the Jerusalem Temple. Our English word *kneel* is derived from the word *knee*.

There are two reasons why, in the context of a blessing, one might wish to touch the ground. First, it is proper to physically demonstrate subservience to the source of all blessings—God. Any person expressing a blessing is merely triggering the blessing whose power originates not with him but with the Creator of our world. It is not a bad idea to demonstrate our awareness of this; getting close to the ground, down on our knees, accomplishes precisely that.

At the same time, saying a blessing, a B'RaCHa, has the virtue of grounding us. It is all too easy, especially for those who are ambitious in their spiritual lives, to sometimes lose sight of life's practicalities. Has my desire for closeness with God caused distance to develop between me and my loved ones? Is my determination to love God with all my heart, soul, and strength causing me to act a little less considerately toward the people among whom I live and work? Is my yearning for a spiritual link with heaven diminishing my joy of living in this wonderful world? As we strive for ever greater closeness to the Creator, we run the risk of getting caught up among the clouds and the stars. Blessings help keep us grounded; they help us keep our feet on the ground, which, as humans, we must do. It is frightfully easy to become so caught up in our work that we lose sight of our real goals and purposes. Blessings help us recall that God made the ordinary, physical world as well as the spiritual one.

I believe it is part of God's plan for us that we should not only jump high, but also—and more than just occasionally—get down on the ground, feel the grass, smell the earth, and thank God for the wonder of Creation. To do this we must set aside time to appreciate the world of ordinary things—thunder and lightning, mountains and oceans, even new clothing or a nice, perfectly yellow banana—just as we set aside time for prayer, meditation, or other more obviously "spiritual" activities.

Another ability that knees give us is jumping. If our knees didn't bend, we couldn't jump or reach for the sky. Every creative, ambitious person is always actively jumping—stretching his body and soul to reach as high as he can. This uniquely human desire of ours to reach for the stars is itself a blessing. Uttering frequent blessings is one way to constantly challenge ourselves to reach beyond the limitations of our own vision. We all remember the old aphorism "Look before you leap." Well, blessings remind us that sometimes the only way to cross the chasm is by leaping, even if the landing site is not visible. Yes, sometimes it is necessary to leap before you look. Knees and blessings, being the same Hebrew word, both remind us of how important it is to be able to jump.

Finally, knees allow us to run. In fact, they are essential for running. Without them, we'd have a hard time indeed moving at a pace much faster than a goose-stepping walk. Notice the way competitive runners crouch at the starting line before a race, their knees bent at the ideal angle to launch them into the race. Running sends one simple signal: urgency. When we see someone running, we know that to him time is short. Well, that also is a message we should each carry with us. The commodity that is in shortest supply is not money, but time.

My late father, who was also my Torah teacher, harbored an intense dislike for card games. I don't think I ever really understood his feelings until my first visit to a Florida retirement community. There I saw many elderly-yet-vital human beings whiling away their final years on earth—playing cards. To my dad, card games suggested that you had all the time in the world—there was no urgency about you.

In my work as an adviser to business executives, I am sometimes asked to evaluate the condition of a company or office. One of the first things I try to measure is the average level of urgency felt by employees and associates in the enterprise. If too many people are gazing out of windows, strolling the hallways, or otherwise exhibiting no sense of urgency, I know that we have a problem.

Knees remind us of our ability to run, and blessings remind us of why we should. Both running and jumping require not only that we have knees, but also that we should be in touch with the ground. You see, if we were suspended in midair we could convulse our leg muscles with all our might but go nowhere. Unless a runner can thrust back against the ground, he will achieve no speed at all. Unless a jumper can launch himself from the firm, unyielding ground, he too will not achieve liftoff. Thus, the fact that the Hebrew word for blessing is also the word for knees helps to tie together the themes of running, jumping, and the ground. Only by being in touch with the ground can we adequately reach for heaven and achieve urgency. Only by correctly using the gift of blessing can we maintain the exquisite tension between our need to be reliably rooted to the ground and our yearning for spiritual completion. To put it as simply as possible, there is built into our nature a human need to join Heaven and Earth.

When a wheelbarrow full of uranium fuel is loaded aboard a nuclear submarine, it is enough to provide propulsion, electricity, air, and water for the vessel and its intrepid crew for about a year. Nobody on board possesses that kind of power within himself, but he does possess the ability to deploy the almost unlimited nuclear power that is hidden in the nuclei of those uranium atoms. By ourselves, we are not very powerful people, either. But we all possess the ability to deploy the almost unlimited power that God has hidden deep within the heart of the blessing.

CHAPTER TWENTY-SIX

Maintaining Our Two Lives in Health

ChaY-iM

חיים

I f you want to know something about other people's inner lives, I advise you to eavesdrop. No, I am certainly not suggesting that you pry into other people's lives, just that you don't block your ears when others talk at the top of their voices.

Often I can hear another airplane passenger, seated three rows back, relating his life story. He is managing to make himself heard above the roar of four large jet engines, and I pity his victim whom I imagine to be trapped in the middle seat.

The other day I overheard an older man going on and on about his health. At great length he was informing another fellow about the peaks of fitness he had attained. He was a recent triathlon participant and was expounding on how, in pursuit of top form for running, swimming, and bicycling, he had limited his intake of dietary fat. "Now," he said, "I hardly eat any fat at all!"

I was amused to hear his listener attempt several times to turn the conversation to other subjects, such as family or a recently published book. However, the speaker remained oblivious to the distress of his audience and doggedly continued listing his vitamin regimen.

The conversation, such as it was, stuck in my mind because this trim athlete is a type of person you meet all the time: the health bore, obsessed with prolonging youthful flexibility beyond all previously held records and determined to tell any listener in considerable detail how he's doing so.

Our society has become quite obsessed with physical safety. I am not opposed to seat belts, bicycle helmets, or food safety inspections, yet I do think that something in our culture is off-kilter when we focus only on physical threats like these. We are rightly concerned about dirty air polluting our lungs, but how about dirty lyrics polluting our souls? When we are more concerned with a cell phone tower being built in our neighborhood than the sexual promiscuity of our high school students, I worry that we have a serious blind spot. This fixation on the physical, as demonstrated by the man at the gym as well as by safety fanatics, interests me because it illuminates the peculiarity of the Hebrew word for "life": *ChaY-iM*. What is unusual about this word is that the *im* at the end signals that it is a plural noun.

Many people wear a necklace with a little pendant at the end consisting of the Hebrew word *chai*, spelled *chet-yud*, which means "life" in the singular sense because it lacks the *im* suffix. But when the Bible speaks of human life, the word used is ChaY-iM, literally "lives." Were an individual to talk in Hebrew about his life, he would grammatically be speaking about his *lives*. Had the talkative athlete in my gym wanted to say in Hebrew, "I've had a long life," he would have had to say, "I have had long lives."

One of the two trees prohibited to Adam in the Garden of Eden was called the tree of life, or in Hebrew, *Etz ha'ChaY-iM*. (Tree is *Etz,* and the *ha* before ChaY-iM functions as the definite article *the*.) Literally, *the tree of lives*.

NOT ONE LIFE, BUT TWO

The Lord's language is telling us quite unequivocally that human beings have not just one life, but two. You wouldn't have known it to listen to that chap in the gym, but this is the whole point. We possess not only a biological life, but also a spiritual one. Most health nuts I've come across fail to realize this. For them, the physical body is the sum total of human existence. So naturally, exercising the body that is the vehicle of their only life becomes the supreme value.

In the Bible we find the word *chai,* the word for (singular) life, in the story of Adam and Eve. Here the first lady of human history is called *em kol chai,* "mother of all life." From this phrase Adam derived the name he gave to his wife: in Hebrew, *Chavah.*

Now I am striving with all my might not to bore you with the technicalities of Hebrew grammar. But you should know that, in turning chai into the name of a woman, as he wished to do, Adam would more naturally have given Eve the Hebrew name *ChaYaH*. This would be the feminine form of the word *ChaY*.

(Transforming a masculine noun, like chai, into its feminine form is typically accomplished by adding an *ah* sound.) Yet Adam introduced a new *v* sound rather than follow the rules. Why? He needed to do this because ChaYaH was already used during the days of Creation to refer to animal life. Adam's point in naming Eve is that there is a very profound difference between animal and human existence. Adam chose the name Chavah, or Eve, to avoid any potential confusion among his descendants.

Animals have only one life, the biological one. Whatever they do is predicated on instinct, not reasoned choice. They certainly have no urge to pray to God or to read an uplifting poem. Indeed, an animal's chief concern is the preservation of its physical self and the production of progeny.

Built into animals is an instinct for self-preservation. As a child growing up in Africa, I often went on family trips to various game preserves. It was amazing to see how careful the wildlife were about protecting their health. Often we would come across elephants drinking from a river, while other elephants rolled around and muddied the waters of the same rivers. No doubt they also relieved themselves there, too. But the elephants never varied their pattern. Whatever they did in the water was always downstream from where they would drink.

By contrast, people in some countries still pollute their own water supplies while in other societies, proper sanitation has been learned and improved over many centuries. Even now, new technologies are being employed. Unlike humans, animals do not build upon generational experience; instead they instinctively do the same thing generation after generation.

MORE THAN THE PHYSICAL

Unlike animals, we humans often risk and endanger our lives for purposes that have nothing to do with physical survival. Only humans risk everything to climb Mount Everest or skydive. Obviously we humans consider some things more important than mere physical survival. On occasion, certain types of animals—for example, dogs—will sacrifice themselves to save their owners. But, other than in fanciful literature, dogs will not gather together and decide to die for an abstract idea. On the other hand, history is replete with accounts of humans willing to die rather than renounce their faith. We see the same noble commitment to ideal over physical survival when men go marching off to battle in order to protect their country.

The point that humans care about more than physical survival is even proven when people risk their lives in pursuit of less worthy goals. We may abuse alcohol and drugs, smoke cigarettes to excess, or challenge a rival in a dangerous activity for the sake of achieving what's called a "high." These goals may be less lofty but they are nonetheless spiritual. I need to stress that *spiritual* is not a synonym for "good" or "holy"; it is merely the opposite of *material*. Patriotism and selfishness, good and evil are all spiritual concepts that cannot be measured with any scientific instruments. Each of these is a nonmaterial concept. Nothing in the physical realm of our existence explains the human need to feel high—elevated, lofty, free of physical constraint. Physical addiction to certain drugs may occur; but the motivation that led the addict to start shooting up or snorting in the first place was spiritual pain, not physical need.

Not for nothing is alcohol sometimes called "spirits." When we get drunk or high, we are seeking a substitute for some lack in our spiritual lives. The resulting buzz is a counterfeit spirituality. But imitation is the highest form of flattery. Drug addicts are a reminder to us of the powerful need we all have to achieve a spiritual high. One can achieve it the ancient and authentic way, by pursuing God, or one can attempt to do so in dangerous and debased ways.

Invariably, people who live their lives with a material orientation are the same people that find themselves attracted to dangerous pursuits. In one way or another the call of the soul will be answered. It is almost as if a little voice goes off saying, "You think that nothing matters except your physical body? Well, now we'll have you do something really risky, say bungee jumping, just so the deepest recesses of your soul will know that you don't really mean that. Your action will now demonstrate that you don't really think your physical safety is all that matters." I do not mean this to sound smug, but those who demonstrate their commitment to spiritual health with the same fervor they dedicate to the physical find far less need to climb snow-clad peaks, jump from airplanes, or for that matter, seek escape from the mind-numbing effects of materialism through drugs or alcohol.

DOING THE MATH

According to the ancient kabalistic study of gematria, where letters correspond to numbers, the sums of various words convey meaning. Examples of gematria are only valid when they have been handed down through the generations; they would be rather meaningless if they were computer generated.

If we add up the letters/numbers in ChaY-iM—*chet, yud, yud, mem*—we get a sum of sixty-eight. This is exactly the number that forms the word for "wise man," *ChaChaM*, whose letters can likewise be added together, producing a figure of sixty-eight. In this case, as in others received through tradition, the equivalent value serves to point out a relationship between the two words ChaY-iM and ChaChaM. In other words, wise people recognize that for humans there are two lives, not just one, and that they need to protect their spiritual as well as their physical lives.

You see, just as there are gyms and pools and running tracks where you can exercise your body, so are there gyms designed to exercise the soul. They are wherever wisdom, as the Bible defines it, is to be found. This would include houses of worship and religious schools but also less formal settings such as the homes of wise clergymen and elders from whom we can learn wisdom.

Will just any wisdom do? Sorry, afraid not.

THE BLUE LAGOON

Try the following thought experiment. Imagine that we were able to replay what I refer to as the *Blue Lagoon* scenario. In this model (named for the very silly Brooke Shields movie) a young boy and girl are placed on a deserted island. They're young, but we leave them plenty of food and shelter to get through their adolescence. The island has plenty of natural resources and no dangerous animals or insects.

Let's assume that we installed clandestine surveillance cameras all over the island, and just sat back and watched for, oh, about four thousand years. What would happen to our pair of Robinson Crusoes? Obviously they would mate, and gradually a human society would appear. Scientific discoveries would be made before long. They would start using fire. Bronze, iron, and eventually steel would appear. They would first produce steam engines, then internal combustion engines, and finally electricity and nuclear power. Why wouldn't these developments occur? Assuming they all survive, these materialistic advances are inevitable. However, assuming they all survive is a mighty big assumption.

But what about God? Remember, the little boy and girl were too young to remember anything about Him from their parents. Will they discover God? Probably not. Like all primitive societies, they will undoubtedly develop superstitions. They will have a vague awareness of a spiritual realm. But there is no reason to think they will develop any consciousness of God. How could they?

Will the island paradise of our thought experiment be a successful society? It will have technology, but will it have real wealth, freedom, or happiness? I don't think so. (Unfortunately there is no way to conduct the experiment for real and find out. Those killjoys at the Society for the Prevention of Cruelty to Children Trapped on Desert Islands would put a stop to it.)

Evidence has been emerging for decades now that "culture" supports civilization. I'm talking about real culture—not opera, novels, ethnic cuisine, or a certain style of joke telling, but rather the web of spiritual values that regulates the behavior of the members of that culture. It has become clear that nations blessed with certain kinds of cultures—those closest to ancient biblical values—do much better at developing and maintaining the sort of institutions that are conducive to a free, tolerant, and wealthy society. The most successful cultures tend to possess, at the core of their intermix of values, an abiding awareness of God. Not just any god, but the God of the Bible.

The Soviets suffered from no shortage of *chay*, life, in the sense of biological life, but they wished to separate it from *chai* with its spiritual meaning. Russia is even now struggling to recover from that terrible error.

It should be just as clear that maintaining this dual aspect of ChaY-iM enhances the effectiveness not only of nations but also of individuals. As my father used to say, "Better a soul without a body, than a body without a soul." When you forget about the soul, the body will be endangered, too.

No one had to explain any of this to Winston Churchill. Now Churchill was a very wise man, but Neville Chamberlain, who preceded him in the role of British prime minister, was smarter. At least he was smarter in the ways that can be measured by IQ tests, SAT scores, and the like. He got significantly better grades in school than did Churchill. But Churchill ended up having to fight World War II and save Britain as well as the rest of Europe because of the grievous blunders that Chamberlain made in foreign policy.

Foremost among these was the latter's appeasement of Hitler. Somehow the brilliant Mr. Chamberlain turned out to be entirely blind to Hitler's wiles. If he had not been so, the terror and suffering of World War II might have been averted. But for all his smarts, Chamberlain was a one-dimensional character. He believed in bodies, not souls. Thus he misread the Fuhrer, who was a very spiritual person— negatively so. The truly evil among us tend to be just that. This is part of the key to their power.

I must stress once again that "spirituality" can be good, or it can be evil. A bad person who lacks a spiritual awareness will never do much worse than petty vandalism and low-grade thuggery. However, a bad person with a highly developed spiritual life can easily become a Stalin or a Hitler. Chamberlain was fooled by Hitler's reassurances that he meant no evil toward Czechoslovakia because the prime minister assumed that Hitler was, more or less, just like him—a body without a soul. Prime Minister Chamberlain assumed that like an animal, Hitler would never do anything that could jeopardize his own physical survival. Wrong! Bad mistake! Animals are not capable of evil and humans obviously are. We call foxes clever, but of course they are not. A fox does what a fox does—for instance, raid a henhouse—purely out of instinct. The cunning duplicity of a Hitler was invisible to Chamberlain. Hitler was committed to ideals, not just to physical survival. Very evil ideals, to be sure, but ideals nonetheless.

TWO LENSES FOR TRUE PERSPECTIVE

An awareness of ChaY-iM in its full meaning can be compared to looking at a distant horizon using binoculars, as opposed to observing the same scene through a telescope. You see the same objects in your field of vision: trees, a house, and a mountain. But with a telescope the element of depth is missing because you are trying to peer at reality through only one lens. Your vision is therefore fatally handicapped. When you use two lenses you can see truth.

We will all benefit from becoming accustomed to viewing every aspect of life through not only one, but two lenses. Using both the material lens along with its equally important spiritual counterpart allows us to make accurate judgments and maintain our two lives in full health.

CHAPTER TWENTY-SEVEN

The Currency of Gratitude

TODaH

תודה

O ne of my most rewarding moments as a rabbi or teacher came during a lecture I was delivering a few years ago to a group of young Jewish professionals in Santa Monica, California. As I usually do, I tried to inject a few pyrotechnic effects into what was quite a technical discussion.

My father taught me to design a speech in the form of a musical symphony. There was to be a theme; there were variations on the theme; there was to be a beginning, a middle, and an end. And at unexpected moments, he insisted, much as the composer Hayden did with his Surprise Symphony, there was to be a flamboyant outburst of conspicuous virtuosity to help hold the audience's attention.

I can't say that I ever lived up to Dad's oratorical skill, but to this day I never prepare a speech or lecture without at least trying to follow his example as well as his stage directions. As I drew close to the end of that particular presentation I began to pull the pieces together for the wrap-up. I had presented a biblical puzzle, dissected it, rotated it for examination from different directions, and ruled out most of the apparent answers. Finally came the moment I always enjoy.

With a flourish worthy of any stage magician, I yanked away the black cloth that had concealed the moral message of the evening and there, hanging almost visibly in the air between us, was the brightly glowing answer to the problem that had perplexed us for nearly ninety minutes.

I glanced around the room to see how many people were enraptured by my presentation. I hoped they would appreciate not only what I had taught, but also how I had presented it. But most of the attendees were regular students of mine and were quite accustomed to my attempts at showmanship, so my glance was met mostly with polite smiles. However, one rather shy and retiring sort of fellow, a business school graduate, was hearing me for the first time. My gaze was immediately drawn to his face in the crowd. His jaw was drooping, his mouth open. He had stopped breathing and was gaping at me through eyes bulging out of his head. Then all the stored up air in his chest came whooshing out of his mouth in one loud, involuntary, monosyllabic exclamation: "Wow!" he yelled.

Horrified at his indiscreet outburst, he turned red and desperately scanned the packed room for an escape route.

"Please don't leave yet," I entreated him. "You can't possibly know how much I appreciate your reaction. I still have to thank you."

He tried to explain himself. "The past hour and a half will assist my business career more than any similar period of time I spent at Harvard Business School," he firmly declared. "But why did you say that you still have to thank me? It seems to me that it ought to be the other way around."

THE IMPORTANCE OF GRATITUDE

This is what I told him.

The Hebrew word for "giving thanks," *TODaH*, also means "to admit, confess, or acknowledge." The reason is pretty clear. By thanking someone for what they gave me or did for me, I am admitting that I needed their contribution. I am acknowledging that prior to their gift I was incomplete. And yes, I am even confessing that I wouldn't be who I now am had they not interceded with deed or gift. This is one reason so many of us find it emotionally difficult to look a benefactor in the eye and utter a sincere "thank you." Deep down we recognize that our expression of gratitude is an eloquent confession that our benefactor has just repaired one kind of shortcoming or another in ourselves.

Expressing gratitude is considered so important in rabbinic tradition that we find the word *TODaH* is actually the root origin for the word *Jew*. The old word for Jewish people is *Juden*. Doubtless you have heard German soldiers screaming this in World War II movies. Juden is the plural, while the singular sounds much more like the original, *Judah*, the fourth son of Jacob. Although the word we use for thanks is TODaH, starting with a *T*, the real root starts with the letter *Yud,* or a *Y* sound, which is exactly how the *J* of Judah transliterates into the Hebrew *Yehuda*—the one who both confesses and gives thanks. Both these actions are good deeds within my tradition. We even have a special day each year called Yom Kippur—the Day of Atonement. Its towering importance in the Jewish calendar is because it is the only day in the year especially reserved for making confession to God. Giving thanks is so important that ingratitude is one of Judaism's major sins.

One of the very first words wise mothers teach their infants is "thanks," or some other baby-appropriate variation. Why do they do this? Is it because Grandpa or Grandma will be offended if the apple of their eye fails to properly thank them for the nice new pink pajamas with a teddy bear on the tummy? No, of course not. Wise Mom knows that for his own future happiness, her baby needs to know how to thank others and to feel comfortable doing so. Adults also need to know this. We thank not because the other party needs our thanks, but because we will be better off for having expressed that gratitude.

We humans experience a corroding of our souls if we are only receivers and not givers. We feel enlarged by giving and diminished by only receiving. This is one of the great tragedies of living on charity, and why the noblest form of charity is to help the recipient become independent of our goodwill as quickly as possible. Paradoxically, humans dependent upon the largesse of others even become resentful. We often find this in teenagers whose bodies and young minds are telling them "I am my own person" and yet, frustratingly, they are still dependent upon their parents. One way of assisting young people through this tough period is to encourage them to earn money in a real job and to praise their fiscal accomplishments when they do so. This helps them bring their urges for independence into line with the realities of life. It can sometimes be valuable for them to even help with some of the family's expenses.

Since being recipients can diminish us, make us feel resentful toward our benefactors, and even corrode our souls, should we then try to avoid receiving things? Absolutely not! That would not only be ungracious toward those of our friends and relatives who may wish to give to us, but it is also quite impossible. Whether we like it or not, we are recipients of the magical gift of life every morning we rise from our beds. Each time we enjoy a wonderful meal or gaze at a spectacular sunset, we are recipients of priceless largesse. Having a daughter's arms flung around one's neck for a good night hug, or spending an evening aboard a small boat in a quiet anchorage are yet more gifts we are happy to receive. Watching a family of black bears loping along a remote beach in British Columbia is yet another wonderful gift. So many gifts! How do we avoid becoming resentful at being such regular recipients of good?

PAY FOR EVERYTHING

The answer is simple, although perhaps not obvious: We try to pay for everything we receive. Walking out of a store without paying for your merchandise hurts you more than it does the store. The proprietor has certainly lost the money to which he was entitled, but he will gradually recover. You, however, have been irreparably reduced. Each time you use that item you are reminded that you are just a recipient. That purloined impulse is a regular reminder that you have no independent existence as a human being and that you are essentially benefiting from charity. (This ignores the fact that the charity was involuntary, which is just another word for theft.) You are forced to acknowledge that you are inadequate to care for yourself but need to depend upon others, either with or without their consent. Naturally, over time, this will corrode your soul and fill you with resentment and self-loathing. Smart people try to pay for everything from which they benefit.

In the same way, enjoying that sunset and all of life's other great gifts without paying for them hurts us, too. But how on earth do we pay for those priceless gifts—and to whom do we pay? The answer is simple: Saying thanks is a currency of human communication. Whom do you thank? Well, that's easy. If it is a gift from a friend, a relative, or a business associate, you obviously cannot take out your wallet and offer to pay for the gift. That would be ungracious and defeat the purpose of the giver. No, you don't need to do anything like that. All you need do is express heartfelt and sincere thanks, either in person or by letter. Gratitude is a currency of human communication. You have now "paid" for the gift you received and are no longer merely a recipient. You are a participant in a transaction of courtesy and friendship. But you are an equal participant, and not only have you not been diminished by receiving the gift, but you have grown from the interaction.

What if the gift is something for which no other human is responsible? A fresh mountain breeze, the sun shining on raindrops caught in a spider's web like diamonds in a tiara—whom do you thank for these? That's easy, too: God. What if you are an atheist? I guess you are out of luck; I don't have anything else to tell you. Each and every day you receive wondrous and enjoyable benefits for which you have not paid and for which you have no one to thank. Of course, this is going to impact you over time.

That store proprietor would have preferred to receive payment from the shoplifter. That the thief will be irreparably harmed by his folly is not really any consolation for the merchant; he would have liked to be paid. Paying for the product would not only have benefited the customer, but it obviously would also benefit the seller. Similarly, while expressing gratitude chiefly benefits the recipient of the gift, it also adds to the richness of life for the donor. Why is this? Well, have you ever had the unhappy experience of putting all you've got into telling a joke to someone and finding yourself greeted by a blank face? I have. In my case, after my punch line, my friend resembled a department store mannequin. You try to explain the punch line to your utterly nonresponsive friend and he interrupts, "I got it, I got it. It's quite funny." But his face is still immobile. Well, he got your joke, so why are you still feeling vaguely dissatisfied?

You felt almost cheated when he did not respond because, in this case, laughter is the currency of human communication. You reached out to another human with a joke. He did not respond. He was the moral equivalent of a shoplifter; he took your merchandise without paying you for it.

Have you noticed how you sometimes force yourself to laugh at someone's joke that you did not really find funny? You may just have written off your forced smile as being polite. However, you were really being much more. You were participating in the loneliness banishing rite of human communication and paying someone for his effort of reaching out to you with his joke. It was another way of saying thank you. It was another way of confessing your own need for human contact.

When you give gifts to others, you enjoy their gratitude too. You wouldn't be offended if they failed to thank you any more than a restaurateur would be offended if a diner left without paying. Fact is, he wouldn't be happy about the omission and neither would you, but offense is not the issue. Part of the deal in these interactions is that the diner is expected to eat and pay and that the beneficiary is to receive and thank.

When we applaud after a theatrical performance or musical concert, we are saying thank you. Yes, of course we paid for the ticket but that only gained us our seat. We now need to pay for the incredible pleasure we just enjoyed and which benefited us beyond our expectations. The appropriate way to do this is by clapping our hands and demanding an encore. There is something churlish about just sitting there without applauding. In fact, it is just like shoplifting.

When we tip a waiter after a good meal, we are also saying thank you. We are acknowledging that without his efforts our meal would have been less. It benefits us more to bestow a tip upon someone who delivered exemplary service than it does him. Saying thank you is an enlarging activity because it is an act of giving. Deriving benefit from the waiter's service without thanking him would deprive him of a small amount of money, but would diminish our very personalities.

Whenever I deliver a speech or a lecture, I look around for the appreciation. It is my applause and my tip. It tells me that I really connected with other human beings and made the world a less lonely place for us all.

"When you let loose that yell of appreciation," I told that Harvard Business School graduate, "you gave me the biggest gift. Naturally, I had to thank you. My fear was that you would leave before I had the opportunity to do so, which would have left me sad and diminished. Now, why don't you join some of us for coffee, and we can continue the discussion." He did and we became great friends. But he never reacted quite the same to anything I said, ever again.

CHAPTER TWENTY-EIGHT

The Way to Peace and Tranquility

ShaLoM

שלו(סמ)

S
hortly before he died in 1981, Nobel Prize winning scientist Max Delbruck delivered a lecture at Cal Tech, which I was privileged to attend. He spoke engagingly about having encountered the already-famous Albert Einstein in one of the elevators of the Planck Institute in Berlin before World War II.

The audience chuckled as Delbruck described how he almost wished for the elevator cables to snap so he could watch Einstein cope with one of his gravity-themed thought experiments suddenly turning terrifyingly practical. I found myself not only educated by the lecture, but also entertained. Delbruck peppered his technical analyses with quotations from poetry and allusions to music. Along with the rest of the audience, I was utterly charmed.

Returning home, I related the lecture to my wife as best I could and told her of my reaction. Not since I had taken leave of the great teachers at my yeshiva had I encountered anyone who related to almost every aspect of the world as seamlessly as did Max Delbruck. With her style of simple directness that has intimidated me from the day we met, my bride wanted to know why I didn't call Delbruck and arrange a private meeting. Trying to explain to her why this was a terrible idea was quite difficult, so I obtained his phone number from a friend in Pasadena and placed the call.

To my astonishment, Dr. Delbruck himself answered the phone. He sounded amused when I described what it was about his speech that enchanted me and he graciously consented to see Susan and me. Our most undisturbed opportunity to talk, he explained, would be if we accompanied him on his weekly hike over the hills behind Pasadena.

The following Tuesday afternoon Susan and I met the distinguished scientist at his modest bungalow near the campus of the California Institute of Technology. As we looked around his library he recounted how the previous evening he had hosted a book club at which he had reviewed a recent bestseller. That evening he would be playing the violin for a chamber orchestra recital. We chatted a while longer, then set off at a brisk clip up the rugged terrain. He climbed so swiftly that I began to fear that I would eventually have to carry the elderly man back to town. After an hour had elapsed, I changed my mind; it was quite clear that he would be carrying me.

The afternoon was unforgettable! We discussed history, biology, popular entertainment, chemistry, literature, geology, atomic physics, photography, politics, and genetics. To be perfectly honest, much of the conversation was not so much a discussion as it was Delbruck talking and Susan and me raptly listening.

"Do your students enjoy the same unbridled curiosity about every facet of the world that you do?" I asked him. He expressed deep concern and was uncharacteristically vehement when, with sad eyes, he assured me that nothing could be further from the truth. Most science students today, he contemptuously exclaimed, expressed almost no interest in anything outside their area of specialization and knew even less. Then, in a prediction that I have come to believe to be increasingly true, he warned that this interdisciplinary illiteracy would eventually threaten American achievement.

Sadly, a few months later, Max Delbruck was gone. But how the memories of that afternoon linger in my mind!

INTERDISCIPLINARY LITERACY

In the years following that memorable afternoon, it became clear to me that most of the great minds of the past also saw no barriers isolating the many different ways of coming to know our wonderful world. An example is one of my heroes, Winston Churchill. What was he? Soldier, journalist, politician, painter, novelist, bricklayer, orator, or world leader? Perhaps he was the last only as a result of the seamless unity of the first seven.

What a pleasure it would have been to sit in on a sociable seventeenth-century evening with these three friends: poet John Milton, architect Christopher Wren, and scientist Robert Boyle. Not only did they happily get along with one another, but they were also comfortable and knowledgeable in each other's areas of expertise. Wren designed St. Paul's cathedral in London and was also a distinguished astronomer. Milton was a theologian, as was Boyle. The latter not only had a law of physics named for him, Boyle's Law, but he also translated the Bible into many languages in his role as the head of the Society for Propagating the Gospel in New England.

Think of Leonardo da Vinci, who was not only a painter and sculptor but also a designer of helicopters! Think of almost any truly great human being and you will find someone who simultaneously developed the many parts of his personality rather than focus on only one narrow area to the detriment of the others.

Have you ever heard some cruel critic calling a computer enthusiast a geek or a nerd? The derision you hear in those words might result from this very point. Certain kinds of males seem to find computers all-absorbing. (Very few females seem to fall victim to this particular form of fascination.) These guys' technical obsessions leave them little time or energy for any other pursuits, so they occasionally strike us as psychically misshapen, almost like a grotesque dwarf with a tiny body and an enormous head. They are very obviously indifferent to almost anything nontechnical while being conspicuously advanced in the one narrow area of digital science.

I suspect that most of us are more comfortable interacting with people with broader interests, which may be why people with intense but narrow interests so often find themselves socially isolated.

ESCAPE FROM OVERSPECIALIZATION

There is escape from this dreadful peril of overspecialization, and it is part of the buried treasure found in the Lord's language.

The Hebrew word *ShaLoM* is the key to welcoming a well-rounded perspective into our lives. It has several meanings, and as always, the treasure lies beneath layers of confusion that conceal how these several meanings really merge into one overarching principle.

These meanings are:

- peace;
- complete;
- pay;
- greetings.

Let us start unearthing the treasure by attempting to combine the first two meanings—peace and complete. Imagine my returning home one evening from work to find an unwashed vagrant, whom I have never seen before, camped on my living-room rug. He has unrolled a smelly sleeping bag and lit a fire in my fireplace. As I walk in, he insolently eyes me and lazily drawls, "Hi."

"Hi, yourself," I might say to him. "You have thirty seconds to get out of this house."

He carefully completes the delicate operation of removing an unappetizing hot dog from the fire before answering. "Stay cool, man. We both want peace, right? I'll keep to my half of the living room, and you can have the other half."

Meanwhile, I am having difficulty trying to decide whether I should resort to my baseball bat or my twelve-gauge shotgun. Sensing my thoughts, he again assures me that he only wants peace. "Let's sit down together and discuss a peaceful solution to our dilemma," he urges me.

This is a gross misunderstanding of the real meaning of peace. Peace is inseparable from its constituent element—completion or totality. I must be made complete or total before we can even begin discussing peace.

In this instance, that vagrant must leave my house and restore me to the condition in which I was before he intruded into my life. Only then can we discuss peace.

This example also happens to reveal how the third meaning, payment, fits in. If a customer takes a pair of shoes from the department store salesman, there is no completion and no peace—just yet. She must first pay for those shoes. That way the store and its salesman are made complete or whole, and then peace can reign. Were she to walk out of the store without paying, there would be little peace. Instead there would be a charge of shoplifting and considerable turbulence for all involved. Peace is far preferable, but can only be attained by all parties achieving totality through payment. Not only does peace depend upon payment for things taken, but it must also be fair—a market-value payment. This is the genius behind the Fifth Amendment to our great American constitution. In it we find the words, "nor shall private property be taken for public use without just compensation."

Our wise founders clearly understood that peace depends upon just compensation. In fact, given the familiarity with Hebrew that many of them enjoyed, it is likely that they also understood that *peace* and *payment* are the same word. Obviously, the fourth meaning—greetings—simply flows from the first three meanings: peace, totality, and payment. When I greet a new arrival or bid farewell to him by uttering the word *ShaLoM,* I am expressing the hope that we shall both enjoy the full tranquility that can only come from totality and discharged obligations or payment.

And it is only the first jewel from the buried treasure chest.

The larger diamond lies just beneath the next shovelful of sand. Again we must examine the first two meanings for ShaLoM—peace and complete. The idea is that peace or tranquility can only come from completion. Here we find the warning against that perilous specialization of personality that Max Delbruck so elegantly avoided.

THE DIFFERENT DEPARTMENTS TO OUR LIVES

We all have different departments to our lives. There is an economic element; we each need a means of generating a revenue stream from which we can satisfy our material needs and desires. We also have an emotional element, which makes us deeply desire the closeness and esteem of other human beings. We have a serious side, and we also have lighthearted and playful aspects to our personalities. Some of us have intense intellectual curiosity about how the world works, and some of us also enjoy a passion for sports. There are those who love nothing more than spending time with their children and those who prefer to be active with communal or service organizations. We can be enthusiastic about our hobbies and about our work. These are just some of the areas that make up a vital, passionate, and fulfilling life.

It is easy to see how quickly we can fall into the trap of expending disproportionate time and energy on only a few of these, while ignoring many others. During my years as a congregational rabbi I encountered one type of unhappy couple more than any other: The wife would beg me to urge her husband to spend less time at work and more time with his young family. Meanwhile, in total frustration, the husband-father hoped I could explain to his tearful wife that he was working so hard only to provide her and their children with the things they needed. She wanted more of his time and attention even if it meant having fewer things. She wanted the balance and peace found only in totality, while he found it easier to focus chiefly upon earning a living.

Then there is the young man who has never been particularly good at sports and discovers computers. All of a sudden they are all that exists in his world. His parents wish he would respond to the call of ShaLoM. *You will only attain true happiness and tranquillity by developing all areas of your being,* they want to tell him. *Get some exercise, meet people—especially girls.* The challenge, then, is to resist the seductive appeal of focusing on only one thing.

I long for the days when we saw this principle at work in the field of medicine. I recognize, of course, that medical science has advanced beyond the point where any one practitioner could possibly know all there is to know; I understand the need for specialists. However, I mourn the vanished general practitioner. How I miss the doctor who viewed me as an entire person! He could see links between different parts of my body: He suspected that my allergy might be linked to the new glasses I recently obtained. He was aware of that infection under a tooth and of my ingrown toenail. He made the broad connections that are tough for a narrow-area specialist to see. He knew the principle of ShaLoM—completeness and totality—the avenue to peace and tranquility.

LINKING THE SPIRITUAL AND THE MATERIAL

The three root letters of the word ShaLoM are the *shin,* the *lamed,* and the *mem*—or *sh, l,* and *m.* The first, the shin שׁ, with its three verticals appearing like tongues of fire reaching for the sky, represents the spiritual. The last, the mem מ, with its womblike shape and its ability to concretize concepts, represents the material. The middle letter, the lamed ל, represents a kind of link between the letter on its right and on its left. It represents learning, assimilation, and understanding, which are perfect metaphors for linking two seemingly disparate concepts.

So at heart the word ShaLoM is saying to us: Do not dream of unlinking the spiritual and the material. It is sheer folly to pursue spiritual reality by isolating ourselves from the material, and it is equally hopeless to pursue the material while completely disregarding the spiritual.

This is why I believe that the best doctors, economists, and engineers are those who also enjoy spiritual understanding. Likewise, I find it most helpful to consult rabbis and other spiritual leaders who have a background in the marketplace or the sciences.

WHAT ARE YOU?

And we should try to avoid all specializations in our daily lives. For instance, we would do better to avoid defining ourselves by just our professions. This is far too limiting for a human being. I have often wondered how to answer the question of what I am. Am I a husband, a father, a rabbi, a writer, a boating enthusiast, a breadwinner, a Bible student, or what? The answer is yes to all of the above.

The message of ShaLoM is that for each of us who seek to live in peace, tranquility, and inner harmony, we have no choice but to evade the tyranny of specialization and to be as much of everything as we can.

Please note that I do not intend this advice to apply to our professional and business lives. There, specialization is absolutely imperative. However, in every other part of life we need to develop ourselves across a broad front. Let us not neglect our roles as parents, but let us also make certain that we don't ignore our roles as spouses and lovers. We must take care of our bodies, and we must also make certain that we constantly exercise our minds and memories. We need to attend to the material realities of our lives, but we should also constantly strive to keep our spiritual flames alight.

Is all of this easy? By no means. It is far more challenging to think of oneself as a whole person than to simply regard oneself as, say, a bond trader, dentist, or janitor. Those may be the ways you earn your living, but they tell me nothing of who you really are.

To get a sense of your completeness—who you really are when you are at peace with yourself—I need to know much more than your business. I want to know your deepest beliefs; I want to know what other human beings share your more private moments; and I want to know what sort of ideas excite you and which enrage you. And that is only a start. You are a complete, exciting, limitless individual, and I would like to get to know you in all your complexity and all your completion.

Which is why, when we meet, I shall extend my hand and say, "ShaLoM."

Multnomah Publishers

The publisher and author would love to hear your comments about this book. *Please contact us at:*
www.multnomah.net/buriedtreasure

One Nation, under God...Indivisible?

YOU ARE IN

AMERICA'S REAL WAR

AN ORTHODOX RABBI INSISTS THAT

JUDEO-CHRISTIAN VALUES ARE

VITAL FOR OUR NATION'S SURVIVAL

RABBI DANIEL LAPIN

ISBN 1-57673-655-5 PB

"Written with passion, wit, and insight."
— Dr. William J. Bennett
author of *The Book of Virtues*

"*America's Real War* is a book which should bring joy to the hearts of Christians and Jews alike. Rabbi Daniel Lapin, in language that is as remarkable for its clarity as for its scholarship and integrity, reveals convincingly that the key to the cultural conflict in America is the moral imperative found in the Judeo-Christian ethic."
— D. James Kennedy, PH.D.
Senior Minister, Coral Ridge Church, Fort Lauderdale, Florida

Now on Audio
Read by Rabbi Daniel Lapin

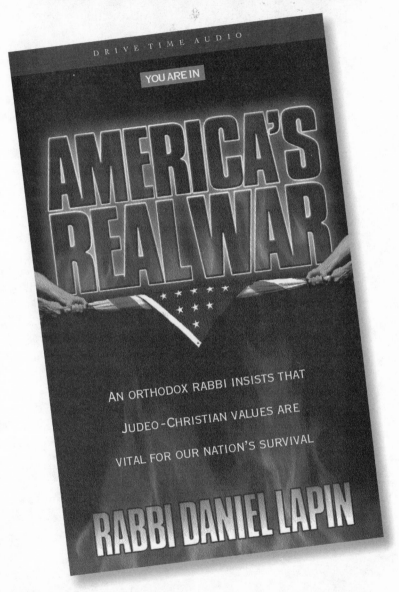

Renowned spiritual leader and speaker Rabbi Daniel Lapin argues that
America was founded on Judeo-Christian values and this tradition is
essential to restoring the country to tranquility, spiritual vitality, and true
greatness.

Drive Time Audio™
ISBN 1-57673-467-6

For more information about **Toward Tradition,**
Rabbi Lapin's foundation for restoring America's greatness,
or to find out about his audio cassettes, mail or fax the form below.

Name_____

Address_____

City_____ State_____ Zip_____

Business Phone_____ Home Phone_____

Fax_____ E-mail_____

❒ Yes, I want information on Toward Tradition

❒ Yes, I want information on Rabbi Lapin's extraordinary
new audio cassette series:

America's Biblical Blueprint

❖   ❖   ❖

A stunning and unforgettable picture of how the Bible has impacted
American history and continues to do so today. The Bible's practical
message to you as you've never heard it before…available
whenever you wish; in your home, your car, even while you exercise!

Whatever your religion—everybody needs a "Rabbi."
Here is your rabbi and teacher in ten spellbinding lectures.
You will feel as if you are in the room with him.

Please mail to: Toward Tradition
P.O. Box 58
Mercer Island, WA 98040

Or Fax to: (206) 236-3288

Or Call us at: (800) 591-7579 or (207) 236-3046

Or E-mail us at: Btaub@towardtradition.org

Check out our web site at www.towardtradition.org